PRINCIPLES OF RAISING

GODLY CHILDREN

PASTOR CLIFF MCANTHONY

TABLE OF CONTENTS

Acknowledgment

I give all glory to God Almighty who brought me to Holiness Revival Movement Worldwide (HOREMOW) and inspired me to organize the special program that eventually gave birth to this book. I thank our LORD and Savior Jesus Christ for the wisdom and grace to accomplish the writing of this book. I thank Pastor Paul Rika, the International Director of HOREMOW, who gave me the opportunity to serve in the capacity that enabled me to organize such programs. May God continue to bless you with the wisdom, knowledge, and understanding needed to lead His great Movement in Jesus' name, Amen. I also want to thank and acknowledge all the wonderful people who attended the special program and whose comments motivated me to write this book. May God continue to bless you all, including those whose comments I have not included in this book. May your blessing increase continually as this book continues to bless lives around the world in Jesus' name, Amen.

Principles of Raising Godly Children was a special program I did on Zoom in 2022. I covered only eight out of the ten principles of raising godly children in the program because of limited time. The attendance was great, and the people were graciously blessed. The comments from the audience were enormous and inspiring. Many commented, please do part 2, and expressed how the program has blessed them. While preparing the lessons for the program, a thought dropped in my heart to make a book out of the program's lessons. I knew it was the LORD and I kept it to heart. At the end of the program, sister Taki of North Dakota suggested that I should turn the lessons into a book. Her comments alongside the text and verbal comments of the attendees became a motivating force that helped birth this book. I have attached a few of the text comments from the special program.

1. Sister Cate – Minnesota, USA: Can there be a part 2, please, by God's grace?
2. Sister Rebecca – North Dakota, USA: My children, no more kids brethren.
3. Sister Taki – North Dakota, USA: This program was a great blessing to us all.
4. Sister Garlorway – North Dakota, USA: Can't wait for this message to be posted on YouTube. Yes part 2 please, as the spirit of the Lord Almighty leads.
5. Sister ZoQueen – Maryland, USA: Parents! You are your child's first teacher!
6. Sister Kenchele – Nevada, USA: Not just COCOMELON, but these children's shows are so hyper-stimulating that it actually acts as a drug, a stimulant. The brain gets a hit of dopamine from

screen time, and it seems that the stronger the "drug" level of stimulation a show delivers, the stronger the "hit". We know there is more behind it spiritually as well.

7. Sister Cate – Minnesota, USA: Absolutely true, my niece is so used to watching all these things on TV when I tell her anything that pertains to Jesus, she says "It's boring".

8. Brother Gabe – Queensland, Australia: May God help all parents discern these digital narcotics!

9. Brother Kingsley – Minnesota, USA: The Lord help us in raising up our children in His word. NO MORE KIDS. THEY ARE CHILDREN OF GOD.

10. Sister Roxann – Ontario, Canada: Wow! I never thought about the rap and hip-hop examples of the name "dog." My! My! My!

11. Sister Kukor – Minnesota, USA: USA: Part 2, please??? We are blessed. God bless you, Pastor Cliff. More grace!!!

12. Sister Vicky – North Dakota, USA: Yes, Part 2 Please. Part 1 was great, Part 2 will be greater in Jesus' Name. To our beloved Pastor Cliff - More anointing and wisdom to you Sir. God bless you.

13. Sister Audris – North Dakota, USA: Thank you, Pastor Cliff. More grace.

Preface

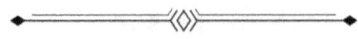

Principles are accepted fundamental (essential, important, central) laws of truth from which expected results are derived or achieved. In other words, "Principles of Raising Godly Children" means; **the essential laws of truth from which raising Godly children can be achieved.** That is, the foundational or primary laws of truth by which raising Godly children is possible. Many Christian parents' goal and desire is to raise godly children who love the Lord and obey Him, children of great decorum. However, without following the principles or the fundamental laws of truth by which this goal could be achieved, their efforts are futile, and their desires are only a mirage. This book explicates ten essential principles of raising godly children for the LORD.

The very first step to training a child is by role modeling. Parents are usually the first role models for their children. You must practice what you want to see in your children. You cannot afford a hypocritical lifestyle before your children if you truly desire to raise godly children. Children give the most attention to the things they observe. They internalize them and mimic them. Once a child is born, his focus is on all the observable cues in the environment, especially those of the parents, as he studies his new world for adaptation. Observation is a child's primary mechanism for learning. When a mother tells his infant child to smile, the child smiles not because he understands the mother's words, but because he sees the mother smiling. Because of this natural skill, children tend to give more attention to what they observe than what they are told. Your children are in your private life, which may not be visible to the public, and they pay close attention to all you do to internalize them and to mimic the same.

Secondly, you must start early, you can easily bend a tree when it is young and tender. However, with time, the same tree becomes rigid, difficult to bend, and even impossible to bend without breaking it. Proverbs 22:6 ***"Train up a child in the way he should go: and when he is old, he will not depart from it."*** The child in this Bible verse refers to children from ages 0-7. King Josiah was raised by his mother to fear and obey the LORD within this age period. He became king at age eight as a godly child and never departed from the way of the LORD until his death. Therefore, you must start training your child at Ground-Zero. Adequate time and resources must be invested in training. Training must be according to sound Biblical principles that prioritize parenting over friendship. Parents must have adequate knowledge and spiritual understanding necessary to protect their children from Satan and destruction.

Early years psychology says, "Give me the child until he is seven and I will make him what you want him to be." This psychology says that ages 0-7 are the formative years of a child's life; that is, character molding-wise. Everything else we do to mold a child's character after age 0 - 7 cannot be foundational and may not last. The philosophy is, "The earlier the better." This is secular psychology. The world and Satan understand this God-given natural principle and take due advantage of it. Unfortunately, most Christian parents disregard this principle. They have named their children goats (Kids) and left them in the hands of Satan to kiddify them through his kiddifying agents.

Satan has deceived parents to leave the most valuable period of training their children in his hands through social media, music, TV, cartoons, video games, and dolls. Has Satan used these devices as kiddifying agents to raise young kids and big kids, that is, young goats and big goats for Christian parents? This book also explores how Satan is influencing parenting through modern culture, using media, music, video games, and dolls to corrupt children. Through these channels, Satan has raised young souls disconnected from God and captivated by worldly influences. Kiddified children—untrained children who do not know God nor care about the things of the LORD. Children who have been turned into spiritual goats and dedicated to Satan for eternal damnation in hellfire. The book expounds on the ten fundamental principles of raising godly children and the efficacy of persistent prayers for our children. May God illuminate the understanding of Christian parents and empower them to take the right actions to save their children from Satan and raise godly children for the LORD. In Jesus's name, Amen.

CHAPTER 1

Model What You Want in Your Children

O nce a child is born, his focus is on all the observable cues in the environment, especially those of the parents, as he studies his new world for adaptation. Observation is a child's primary mechanism for learning. Although a child may not understand your language in infancy. Nevertheless, they are cognitive enough to understand and respond to environmental and human cues. When a low pleasant sound of music is playing, a child understands that this is soothing and tends to relax and sleep. But when a harsh and noisy sound plays, the child will react in the opposite direction, get agitated, and cry to express his displeasure or fear. When a parent tells his infant child to smile, the child does not understand the parent's language. Nonetheless, the child smiles, not because of the word but because he sees the parent smiling.

This observational skill of the child will continue to be the predominant learning skill set for the child, right from infancy through childhood. Because of this natural skill, children tend to give more attention to what they observe than what they are told. Your children are in your private life, which may not be visible to the public, and they pay good attention to all you do to internalize and mimic the same. Therefore, you cannot afford to be a parent whose private life or actions belie the virtues and moral principles you proclaim in public, teach and expect of your children; if you truly want to raise godly children.

1.1: The Significance of Parental Role Modeling

Consciously or unconsciously to parents, their' everyday life is role modeling for their children. You cannot afford to be a hypocrite before your children if you truly desire to raise godly children. Children give the most attention to the things they observe, to internalize them, and to mimic them. Model what you want to see in your child. For example, you cannot tell your child that telling lies is wrong, yet he sees you telling lies. That child will have trouble telling the truth for the rest of his life. Just like telling a child to tell a visitor that you probably don't want to see, "tell him I am not around". How do you expect such a child to speak truthfully in his life? You cannot tell your child that praying is good, but you are not praying. At their foundational age, they want to do everything they see you do. Children see the world through their parents. So, whatever they see their parents practice is what they will emulate. If you want your children to read their Bibles, let them see you read yours often. If you want to train your child to attend church and you are not going to church yourself, your training is in vain. If you want to train your child to be attentive during church service. Then he or she should not see you inattentive when you are in church service. Your child sees you not taking the presence of God seriously, and yet you want them to fear God? No! They will treat God and church services worse than they observed you treat them.

Why Your Infant Child Fights for Your Smartphones And iPads

It is often hilariously said that the 21st-century child starts seeking and fighting for smartphones and iPads right from birth. Why is this so? The Igbo tribe in Nigeria has an adage that says, "Truth is often told amid jokes." Although it is jokingly said that the first thing the 21st-century child seeks right from birth is smartphones and iPads. However, a very important truth is entrenched in it. These children tend to gravitate towards electronic gadgets because that is what they observed their parents doing most of the time. The first time a child opens his eyes in the hospital bed, with great excitement, the mother picks up the iPad or smartphone to take pictures. She takes pictures or records videos of the child and herself for keeps, or posts on social media with the caption "Oh! he is so cute." The parents come home with the child, and when he cries, the iPad or smartphone is up for videos and pictures. The child laughs, and the iPad or smartphone is up again for videos and pictures. When he opens his eyes in the cradle, the parents are busy with their smartphones or iPads. While he is being breastfed, the mother is busy with her smartphone, either talking or on social media.

The child observes all these, internalizes them, and concludes without saying a word that the most important things in life are these electronic gadgets. That is why they have been fighting for your smartphones and iPads since infancy. It is what they have observed their parents do and are eager to do the same. The child's desires will gravitate towards what they see you do often. That's why they started fighting for your smartphones or iPads almost immediately after birth. Always remember that your lifestyle will most likely become their lifestyle on steroids. Imagine what the outcome would be. If parents consistently demonstrate in practice and character all the godly virtues they want to see in their children, right from their infancy. Their godly lifestyle will eventually become the children's godly lifestyle by standards superior to their parents'.

Proverbs 22:6

"Train up a child in the way he should go: and when he is old, he will not depart from it."

The Bible says to train up a child in the way he should go, and when he is old, he will not depart from it. The very first step to training up a child is by role modeling the godly virtues you want to see in your child. Parents are usually the first role models for their children. As parents, you must characterize the virtues you would like to see in your children. You must be a living role model of those godly virtues for your children to observe, internalize, and mimic.

1.2: Biblical Case Study of Godly Parental Role Modeling

Timothy had genuine faith in Christ and became the successor of Apostle Paul in ministry. This did not happen as a fluke, there is a history behind it. Timothy's grandmother, Lois, and his mother, Eunice, practiced the genuine faith that Paul noticed in Timothy. His grandmother and mother's faith in Christ was genuine through observable evidence that Timothy could see from childhood, which he internalized and practiced, even at a scale greater than his parents'.

2Timothy 1:5

When I call to remembrance the unfeigned (genuine) faith that is in thee, which dwelt first in thy grandmother Lois, and thy mother Eunice; and I am persuaded that in thee also.

If the genuine faith found in Timothy was from his grandmother and mother. Then it is certain that he must have observed them because faith can only be known through our works (practices) and not just by verbal utterances. This was why Apostle Paul said with assurance that he was persuaded that the same genuine faith is also in Timothy. Paul concluded that Timothy's grandmother and mother had genuine faith because he could see the fruits (works) of their faith. He knew that children learn, mimic, and adapt through observation, and he was persuaded that Timothy became what he observed in his mother and grandmother.

James 2:17-20

[17]Even so faith, if it hath not works, is dead, being alone. [18]Yea, a man may say, Thou hast faith, and I have works: shew me thy faith without thy works, and I will shew thee my faith by my works. [19]Thou believest that there is one God; thou doest well: the devils also believe, and tremble. [20]But wilt thou know, O vain man, that faith without works is dead?

Timothy's grandmother and mother's faith would not have been able to impart Timothy's life if it were dead, that is, without works (observable evidence). One's faith cannot be observed without works. The believer's faith is seen and proved by their daily observable practices (works), character, and lifestyle. James 2:18 *"Yea, a man may say, Thou hast faith, and I have works: shew me thy faith without thy works, and I will shew thee my faith by my works."* Many people claim to have faith in Jesus Christ (believers) but have no works. The Bible says that such faith is dead and just as good as the faith the devil has. The devil is also a believer in Christ and trembles. James 2:19 *"**Thou believest that there is one God; thou doest well: the devils also believe, and tremble.**"* The devil believes that Jesus Christ is the Son of God and that all powers have been given to Him; that is why he trembles.

Matthew 28:18

And Jesus came and spake unto them, saying, All power is given unto me in heaven and in earth.

Ephesians 1:18-22

[18]The eyes of your understanding being enlightened; that ye may know what is the hope of his calling, and what the riches of the glory of his inheritance in the saints, [19]And what is the exceeding greatness of his power to us-ward who believe, according to the working of his mighty power, [20]Which he wrought in Christ, when he raised him from the dead, and set him at his own right hand in the heavenly places, [21]Far above all principality, and power, and might, and dominion, and every name that is named, not only in this world, but also in that which is to come: [22]And hath put all things under his feet, and gave him to be the head over all things to the church,

The devil has this knowledge and faith (believer) in Jesus Christ as the Almighty God. However, he has no works of righteousness (dead faith). This was not the kind of faith Timothy's grandmother and mother had. Their faith was in the demonstration of godly virtues, which were clearly seen by Timothy and replicated in his life as observed by Apostle Paul.

2Timothy 3:14-15

[14]But continue thou in the things which thou hast learned and hast been assured of, knowing of whom thou hast learned them; [15]And that from a child thou hast known the holy scriptures, which are able to make thee wise unto salvation through faith which is in Christ Jesus.

Whatever your children observe you doing will ultimately form the foundation of their character and life. They will most likely continue in them and not depart from them. They will hold fast to them because they are confident in whom they learned them from. They will not depart from them because they learned/copied them from the most trusted person in their life – their parents. 2 Timothy 3:14 *"But continue thou in the things which thou hast learned and hast been assured of, knowing of whom thou hast learned them;"* Parents are usually the first role models for their children. You must practice what you want to see in your children. They most likely will not depart from them when they grow. 2Timothy 3:15, *"And that from a child thou hast known the holy scriptures, which are able to make thee wise unto salvation through faith which is in Christ Jesus."* The genuine faith and commitment Pastor Timothy had in Jesus and His Word took root in his childhood. Glory to God Almighty for his non-hypocritical Christian grandmother and mother who were godly role models in his life.

CHAPTER 2

Start Training at Ground-Zero (Age 0)

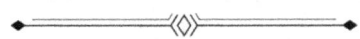

Start training your child at age zero. Training must begin at Ground-Zero, in the foundational stage of character molding (ages 0-7) to be most effective and lasting. Most parents do not start training their children from age zero. They presume that they are too small or not cognitively advanced enough to learn. This is just ignorance on the part of the parents. When the Bible says: ***"Train up a child in the way he should go: and when he is old, he will not depart from it."*** The child there refers to children from ages 0-7. This is the foundational stage of character molding. King Josiah was raised by his mother to fear and obey the Lord within this age period. He became king at age eight as a godly child and never departed from the way of the LORD all the days of his life.

2Kings 22:1-2

¹Josiah was eight years old when he began to reign, and he reigned thirty and one years in Jerusalem. And his mother's name was Jedidah, the daughter of Adaiah of Boscath. ²And he did that which was right in the sight of the LORD, and walked in all the way of David his father, and turned not aside to the right hand or to the left.

2.1 The Intellect of a Child

Most parents do not really understand how intelligent a child is. They often view the child from an adult perspective: how much knowledge they have about things and their level of reasoning. Then they conclude that the child is just ignorant. Yes, they are correct that the child is ignorant. However, ignorance does not mean the child is unintelligent or cognitively impaired, it just means that the child doesn't know much. Obviously, the child does not know much; he just arrived in a new world and must be attentive to observe and learn various skills that will enable him to adapt to his new world. Just imagine yourself as an adult suddenly disappearing from this known world and finding yourself in an alien world. You will be confused and ignorant of all that is going on there. The aliens will also view you as just ignorant. However, this will not mean that you are unintelligent or cognitively impaired. It just means that you don't know much and need much data (knowledge) and time to understand things and adapt to your new world. Now, you are in this alien world, you do not understand their language, and most things going on there. In this condition, all you will give attention to is learning, observing, and processing everything you see to gain some understanding. Imagine how much more you would learn things properly if any alien were kind enough to give you attention and sacrifice time to teach you things and proper decorum. This is the condition that newborns find themselves in. Though they do not know much (ignorant), they are not unintelligent or cognitively impaired. The children are eager to observe and learn. All they need is an adult who will be kind enough to give them attention and teach them decorum and godliness.

Early years psychology says, "Give me the child until he is seven years old, and I will make him what you want him to be." This psychology says ages zero to seven are a child's formative years; character molding-wise. Everything else we do to mold a child's character after they turn seven cannot be foundational and may not last. The philosophy is, "The earlier, the better."

Early years psychology says a child's formative years are from zero to seven years. Anything after that cannot be foundational and will likely not last. And this is where many Christian parents fail. They neglect training their children in their formative years, thinking they are too young to be taught the things of God or the principles of life. Then, when the children grow up astray, they start blaming the children and often abuse them in their effort to correct them.

When I was in Nigeria, there was a period when I lived with an uncle who later traveled abroad for greener pastures. I was then living with his wife and newly born daughter. I noticed that his wife was very lenient with their daughter to a fault. When their daughter started crawling, I observed that her mother removed all the ceramic decorations or breakable things in the living room. She removed anything in the living room that she thought her daughter could break or destroy.

I often corrected her and advised her to teach her daughter to adapt to her environment and make her understand what to touch and what not to touch. But she will always say that her daughter was just a child. I was busy most days and did not spend much time at home. But when I did, I made sure I trained this little girl. If she crawls to the TV or to any other property that is not right for her to play with and touches it. I would gently spank her little fingers and change the countenance on my face. Then she would look at my face, and of course, it wasn't pleasant, then she would start crying. This continued for a while, and with time, she understood her boundaries, at least whenever I was at home. She was able to learn at about seven months when she was still crawling that there are boundaries in life. She was smart enough to learn that there are things she should not do, and places she should not go. If I happened to be in the living room and she crawled to the TV or to any other place I had forbidden her, or where she was not sure if she was allowed to go to, or touch. She would stop, turn, and look at me to see the expression on my face. If I changed my countenance to a frown, she would understand that she is not supposed to touch it or crawl further. She will immediately change direction and move on to something else. But if I smile at her, she will smile back and continue with her intended business.

The little girl learned discipline and to reverence me from the gentle redirection and training that I gave her at that tender age. By the time she was six years old, having been under my discipline and training, she learned to obey me in everything. Whenever I ask her to stop or sit down, she knows to do so immediately. She took all of my instructions seriously. But for her mother, she had no reverence for her. Before her mother could finish giving her an instruction, she would object with NO! Then her mother would pounce on her with her hands in anger, forgetting that she did not train her correctly in the first place. She had trained her daughter not to fear or reverence her and taught her that there are no boundaries in life without saying a word. She trained her daughter to be stubborn and rebellious to her without intending to do so. She Kiddified her daughter without calling her kid (goat). This stresses the fact that you could still kiddify a child without calling them a kid (goat). Whenever parents view their child from the perspective that he or she is just a child, as an excuse for not disciplining them early and promptly. It is the same with he's just a kid (goat) mentality. The only difference is that they did not refer to the child as a kid (goat). Nonetheless, their mentality is still the same goat-like skewed perspective that the child is too young to be trained. Whenever parents fail to train their children appropriately at the foundational stage. They have unknowingly succeeded in training them to be stubborn and rebellious. They have created a vacuum for the death-giving goat spirit to enter their children – the spirit of stubbornness and rebellion. The parents themselves have become tools in the hands of Satan to kiddify their children.

Now that her daughter has grown to be six years old without any foundational training from her. She was now trying to set boundaries and exercise authority over her daughter. Her actions left her daughter confused, instead of learning anything. The girl knew there were no boundaries with her growing up, and her thoughts would be: How come mom is acting like this now? How come she is now saying you cannot do this or that? What has come over her? This is why she was rebellious to her mother. Her mom wanted to reap what she did not sow in her. She wasted her opportunity to train her daughter and discipline her during the foundational years, claiming she was just a child. Unknowingly to her, she was a kiddifying agent in the hands of Satan for the kiddification of her daughter.

Children are intelligent and smart, even from a very tender age. Take, for example, a child who is still breastfeeding. Most often, when they start developing their first teeth, their mother's nipples are in trouble. If the child bites her nipple and she claims he is just a child, the child will keep biting. However, the child will remember not to do it again if the mother corrects him with a gentle smack a few times. The child will quickly learn that biting mom while sucking is not an acceptable behavior. Children from zero to seven do not know much, they are ignorant, nevertheless, they are intelligent. They are like empty containers that will accept whatever their parents pour into them. Therefore, pour godly training into their lives and leave no vacuum for Satan to kiddify them.

Training must begin at Ground-Zero at the foundational stage of ages 0 – 7 to be most effective and lasting. Early years psychology says, "Give me the child until he is seven and I will make him what you want him to be." This psychology says ages zero to seven are the formative years of a child's life; that is, character molding-wise. Everything else parents do after ages 0 – 7 to mold the character of a child cannot be foundational and may not last. The philosophy is, "The earlier the better." This is secular psychology. The world and Satan understand this God-given natural principle and take due advantage of it. Proverbs 22:6 ***"Train up a child in the way he should go: and when he is old, he will not depart from it."***

2.2: Satan's Strategies to Lay Your Children's Foundation

Unfortunately, while Christians treat the Word of God with levity, Satan does not. Satan believes the Word of God, and he is fully aware that not one jot of God's Word will go unfulfilled. Satan understands that the Word of God is effective and eternal.

Matthew 5:18

For verily I say unto you, till heaven and earth pass, one jot or one title shall in no wise pass from the law, till all be fulfilled.

Satan knows that the Word of God is true and forever settled in heaven. **Psalm 119:89 "Forever, O LORD, thy word is settled in heaven."** Satan knows that God's Word cannot fail and that every biblical principle is true and effective. He knows that the foundation of the entire existence of the world and life hangs and thrives on God's Word.

Hebrews 1:1-3

¹God, who at sundry times and in divers manners spake in time past unto the fathers by the prophets, ²Hath in these last days spoken unto us by his Son, whom he hath appointed heir of all things, by whom also he made the worlds; ³Who being the brightness of his glory, and the express image of his person, and UPHOLDING ALL THINGS BY THE WORD OF HIS POWER, when he had by himself purged our sins, sat down on the right hand of the Majesty on high;

Hebrews 11:3

Through faith we UNDERSTAND THAT THE WORLDS WERE FRAMED BY THE WORD OF GOD, so that things which are seen were not made of things which do appear.

God upholds all things He created by the Word of His power. The foundation of the world and life are formed and sustained by the invisible Word of God. Godliness in a family, society, nation, and holy Christian living starts at the foundation of life. Satan knows this, and for the reason to stop godliness and destroy Christianity in the world. He knew well to start from the foundation by hindering parents from raising godly children. The Satanic Ten Points Agenda to destroy Christianity and usher in a new world order by the infamous Satanist Alice A. Bailey started with the children. The Ten Points Agenda was created by Satan to destroy the Christian Worldview. And create a moral shift in belief and lifestyle to birth the culture that will eventually usher in the reign of the Anti-Christ.

ALICE A BAILEY'S TEN POINTS AGENDA FOR NEW WORLD ORDER

1. TAKE GOD AND PRAYER OUT OF THE EDUCATION SYSTEM
2. REDUCE PARENTAL AUTHORITY OVER THE CHILDREN
3. DESTROY THE JUDEO-CHRISTIAN FAMILY STRUCTURE OR THE TRADITIONAL CHRISTIAN FAMILY STRUCTURE
4. IF SEX IS FREE, THEN MAKE ABORTION LEGAL AND MAKE IT EASY
5. MAKE DIVORCE EASY AND LEGAL, FREE PEOPLE FROM THE CONCEPT OF MARRIAGE FOR LIFE
6. MAKE HOMOSEXUALITY AN ALTERNATIVE LIFESTYLE
7. DEBASE ART, MAKE IT RUN MAD
8. USE MEDIA TO PROMOTE AND CHANGE MINDSETS
9. CREATE AN INTER-FAITH MOVEMENT

10. GET GOVERNMENTS TO MAKE ALL THESE LAWS AND GET THE CHURCH TO ENDORSE THESE CHANGES.

Take God and Prayer Out of the Education System

The first point is to remove God and prayer from the education system. This is primarily targeted at children. Alice Bailey explains that if people grow up without reference to God, they will consider God irrelevant in their day-to-day lives. Satan knew that he would not succeed with his agenda to overthrow Christianity, that is, godliness, and usher in the New World Order of life as long as the children were being taught the Word of God and prayers in schools. The children will grow up with some knowledge of God's Word and the fear of God, and will learn to believe and trust God, which will form the foundation of their life, character molding-wise. Therefore, Satan strategized to subtly remove God's Word and prayer from the foundational stage of their life and replace them with secular and anti-God knowledge. Satan knows that the children will not depart from his desired lifestyle if he succeeds in shaping them in knowledge and character at the foundational stage –Ground-Zero, (ages 0–7). Everything else people do to mold children's character after ages zero to seven cannot be foundational and may not last. The philosophy is, "The earlier the better." The world and Satan understand this God-given natural principle and take due advantage of it. Proverbs 22:6 ***"Train up a child in the way he should go: and when he is old, he will not depart from it."***

Why is Satan desperately after the children? Because he knows that if he could capture the children, then he would have captured the human race. He knows children will not depart from the godless foundation he would have laid in their lives. Alice Bailey said, "If the people grew up without reference to God. Then they will consider God irrelevant in their day-to-day life." Has Satan succeeded? If you carefully observe most people born within the last fifty years in first-world countries like the United States, Canada, Australia, Europe, and so on, you will see that this has happened. God has become irrelevant in most people's day-to-day life. The most unfortunate thing is that it is almost impossible to get people who grew up with this marred and corrupted foundation to understand God in a true Christian sense. Even when they do, at some point, they are most likely to fall back and align with the foundation that was already laid in their life. Only through special divine mercy and intervention from the Almighty God will one ever see a different outcome. The above statement may be hard to accept now, however, understanding will come as you read on; let's move forward.

Reduce Parental Authority Over the Children.

Alice Bailey further explained, "Break communication between parents and children so that parents cannot pass on spiritual values to their children. Do this by pushing excessive child rights." If you live in the Western world, you would perfectly understand this and know how and why children got to be given unprecedented rights over their parents by the government. The agenda behind those excessive child rights in most of the Western world is to break the communication between parents and children. Satan achieves this by weakening and destroying parental authority over their children by enacting excessive child rights and laws. The child is then programmed like a robot with these child rights starting from their daycare. The child is thought to report their parents to the school authority for emotional abuse anytime their parents yell at them, or rebuke/scold them. And to call the police for physical abuse if they are flogged or feel threatened by their parents. Satan is the brain behind it all because he wants to have your children at the foundational stage, ages 0 –7, so that he can lay the foundation of their lives unchallenged, with everything secular and anti-God.

Satan knows that the foundation determines the outcome of the structure. "Give me the child until he is seven and I will make him what you want him to be." Everything else done after ages zero to seven to mold the character of the child cannot be foundational and may not last. "The earlier the better." This is secular psychology. The world and Satan understand this God-given natural principle and take due advantage of it. Proverbs 22:6 ***"Train up a child in the way he should go: and when he is old, he will not depart from it."*** Satan knows that God's Word cannot fail and that every biblical principle is true and effective. Therefore, he exploits this biblical truth and principles to establish his evil agenda. While Christians continue to trivialize the same Word of God that was so powerful to bring man and the entire creation into being and to sustain them.

2.3: The Significance of Life's Foundation

The foundation of a building is what determines and sustains the structure to be erected. The foundation determines the weight, size, and design that can be erected. It is the primary power source of resistance for any structure. Structures built on faulty or marred foundations cannot withstand the opposing forces of the natural elements. Errors made at any level of construction are easier to correct so that they align with the foundation laid.

However, if the foundation is faulty, it simply means that the structure cannot stand, and correcting it is to bring down the entire structure and the foundation. It will be a futile effort to lay a weak foundation for a bungalow while laboring to build a skyscraper on it. The foundation laid determines the capacity and shape/design of the structure that could be erected and the power of its resistance against unfriendly natural and manmade adversities. Jesus spoke about the significance of a good solid foundation.

Luke 6:48-49

⁴⁸He is like a man which built an house, and digged deep, and laid the foundation on a rock: and when the flood arose, the stream beat vehemently upon that house, and could not shake it: for it was founded upon a rock. ⁴⁹But he that heareth, and doeth not, is like a man that without a foundation built an house upon the earth; against which the stream did beat vehemently, and immediately it fell; and the ruin of that house was great.

In the same vein as a parent, you are building a house (life) of eternal value, far more important than a structure of bricks and wood. Proverbs 22:6 *"Train up a child in the way he should go: and when he is old, he will not depart from it."* To train up is to build the child's life. You will have to dig deep into that child's life and lay his or her foundation on the solid Rock, which is Jesus – God's Word. Your efforts to build your child's life and raise a godly child will be futile if you are building on a weak, marred (corrupted), or wrong foundation. That is, a foundation laid upon the wrong or corrupted gospel, philosophies of men, false religion, secularism, and anti-God knowledge. This is the reason why the Lord said: *If the foundations be destroyed, what can the righteous do?* Psalms 11:3. I believe by now you can understand why I made this statement earlier: *"The most unfortunate thing is that it is almost impossible to get people who grew up with this marred and corrupted foundation to ever consider God in the true Christian sense. Even when they do, at some point, they are most likely to fall back and align with the foundation that was already laid."* God said it Himself, that the efforts of the righteous, be it of the preacher, the parents, or the child, are futile if the foundation is destroyed. Psalms 11:3 *"If the foundations be destroyed, what can the righteous do?"* Now can you understand the significance of a child's foundation? Therefore, you must labor hard as parents, paying whatever costs and sacrifices necessary to lay a solid foundation for your children. That is, a foundation built on the truth of God's Word.

It is of the utmost importance that you give it your all to lay a good solid foundation for your children. The great thing about it is that they will not be able to depart from it. Proverbs 22:6 *"Train up a child in the way he should go: and when he is old, he will not depart from it."* If you succeed in digging deep to lay the foundation of your child's life on the truth of the gospel, and not on another gospel. Even if the child deviates through external influences from relatives, schools, friends, and social media as he or she grows up. Every wrong structure erected on that child will not fit in and will eventually collapse because a solid godly foundation has already been laid. Think of it this way, you are building a house and you laid a foundation for a rectangular structure, and someone else comes and starts to build a circular structure on it. It will not fit in, and when he realizes himself, he will destroy the wrong structure and follow the pattern of the foundation that was laid. If he does not stop and continues with the wrong structure, it is only a matter of time before the entire thing will collapse. He will then start afresh to build the right structure in compliance with the foundation already laid. This was the case in the story of the prodigal son.

Luke 15:11-19

11And he said, a certain man had two sons: 12And the younger of them said to his father, Father, give me the portion of goods that falleth to me. And he divided unto them his living. 13And not many days after the younger son gathered all together, and took his journey into a far country, and there wasted his substance with riotous living. 14And when he had spent all, there arose a mighty famine in that land; and he began to be in want. 15And he went and joined himself to a citizen of that country; and he sent him into his fields to feed swine. 16And he would fain have filled his belly with the husks that the swine did eat: and no man gave unto him. 17And when he came to himself, he said, How many hired servants of my father's have bread enough and to spare, and I perish with hunger! 18I will arise and go to my father, and will say unto him, Father, I have sinned against heaven, and before thee, 19And am no more worthy to be called thy son: make me as one of thy hired servants.

The prodigal son did not stop building the wrong structure until the whole thing collapsed. He was able to come to himself and realize that his life now does not fit into the foundation of his life. Then he said, I will arise and return to my father, that is, return to my foundation and start to build afresh, Hallelujah! Glory to God Almighty. *Luke 15:17-19: And when he came to himself, he said, How many hired servants of my father's have bread enough and to spare, and I perish with hunger! I will arise and go to my father, and will say unto him, Father, I have sinned against heaven, and before thee, And am no more worthy to be called thy son: make me as one of thy hired servants.* Imagine if he had no such godly foundation. He would not have been able to have any standard for measurement to compare his present life's condition to understand that he is off course. He would have seen his present life's condition as normal and would have continued to build on it to his final doom.

2.4: The Impact of King Josiah and King Joash's Early Childhood Upbringing

There is a great difference in how King Josiah and King Joash were raised at the foundational stage of their upbringing – the character-formative stage of ages zero to seven. King Josiah's childhood upbringing caused him to end well, while that of King Joash caused him to end badly. Their childhood upbringing played a decisive role in the outcomes of their lives. Proverbs 22:6 *"Train up a child in the way he should go: and when he is old, he will not depart from it."*

King Josiah's Early Childhood Upbringing

King Josiah was raised by his mother and received godly training that formed the foundation of his life, which he could not depart from, all the days of his life. He was raised to fear and obey the LORD within the foundational stage of ages zero to seven. He became king at age eight as a godly child and never departed from the way of the Lord all the days of his life.

2Kings 22:1-2

¹Josiah was eight years old when he began to reign, and he reigned thirty and one years in Jerusalem. And his mother's name was Jedidah, the daughter of Adaiah of Boscath. ²And he did that which was right in the sight of the LORD, and walked in all the way of David his father, and turned not aside to the right hand or to the left.

King Josiah was trained by his mother, Jedidah, to be a God-fearing child. That is why the mother's name was referenced instead of the father's. It was to reveal the person responsible for the outcome of King Josiah's character. We can also see similar references in the Bible for Pastor Timothy and King Ahaziah, who did evil.

2Timothy 1:5; 3:14-15

¹:⁵When I call to remembrance the unfeigned (genuine) faith that is in thee, which dwelt first in thy grandmother Lois, and thy mother Eunice; and I am persuaded that in thee also. ³:¹⁴But continue thou in the things which thou hast learned and hast been assured of, knowing of whom thou hast learned them; ³:¹⁵And that from a child thou hast known the holy scriptures, which are able to make thee wise unto salvation through faith which is in Christ Jesus.

Timothy's grandmother, Lois, and mother, Eunice, were referenced as the people who influenced and trained Timothy to be established in the faith. What made Timothy steadfast in the faith and stand out from the corruption and moral decline that plagued the ministers and believers in his days is made clear in 2 Timothy 3:15 *"And that from a child thou hast known the holy scriptures, which are able to make thee wise unto salvation through faith which is in Christ Jesus.* " He was taught the faith from childhood (age 0-7) by his grandmother and mother. They laid a solid godly foundation that he could not depart from all the days of his life.

2Chronicles 22:2-4

2Forty and two years old was Ahaziah when he began to reign, and he reigned one year in Jerusalem. His mother's name also was Athaliah the daughter of Omri. 3He also walked in the ways of the house of Ahab: for his mother was his counsellor to do wickedly. 4Wherefore he did evil in the sight of the LORD like the house of Ahab: for they were his counsellors after the death of his father to his destruction.

King Ahaziah's mother, Athaliah, was referenced as the one who schooled him in evil and sustained him with counsel on how to prosper in evil. A child will always follow and build on the foundation laid in his or her life, whether good or evil. Athaliah laid a solid evil foundation for her son Ahaziah, which he could not depart from all the days of his life. Parents, please sacrifice all that is necessary to lay a godly foundation for your children. You will never regret it. Your sacrifice will bless your life, and family, and bless humanity. King Josiah's mother must have sacrificed so much to ensure that Josiah was raised a God-fearing young man. It was all within the ages of zero to seven – the foundational stage in child training. He never departed from that foundation all the days of his life.

2Kings 22:1-2

1Josiah was eight years old when he began to reign, and he reigned thirty and one years in Jerusalem. And his mother's name was Jedidah, the daughter of Adaiah of Boscath. 2And

he did that which was right in the sight of the LORD, and walked in all the way of David his father, and turned not aside to the right hand or to the left.

King Josiah grew up with his mother, who did not give him away to nannies and daycares to waste his foundational age of character molding. She sacrificed time and resources to teach and train her son. She did not allow another to lay a wrong foundation in his life; she protected him and laid the godly foundation she desired to see in his life. She got what she desired and labored for in works and prayers. It is said that "money corrupts, and power corrupts absolutely," but not King Josiah. Although he had both money and power, and must have faced great temptations to do wickedly at a very young age. Yet he failed not, because his mother had laid a solid godly foundation in his life. King Josiah never departed from the godly foundation his mother laid all the days of his life. Proverbs 22:6 ***"Train up a child in the way he should go: and when he is old, he will not depart from it."*** Glory to God Almighty who is able to keep that which is committed into His hands.

King Joash's Early Childhood Upbringing

In contrast to King Josiah's early childhood upbringing, King Joash did not have a godly mother or father to train him. King Joash was nursed up and not trained. He was given to a nurse at his foundational stage of ages zero to seven to nurse him up, that is, to raise him just like you would raise chickens. The nurse was there to feed and nourish him; it does not require training, but to ensure he is well fed, kept healthy, clean, and happy.

2Chronicles 22:10-12

¹⁰But when Athaliah the mother of Ahaziah saw that her son was dead, she arose and destroyed all the seed royal of the house of Judah. ¹¹But Jehoshabeath, the daughter of the king, took Joash the son of Ahaziah, and stole him from among the king's sons that were slain, and put him and his nurse in a bedchamber. So Jehoshabeath, the daughter of king Jehoram, the wife of Jehoiada the priest, (for she was the sister of Ahaziah,) hid him from Athaliah, so that she slew him not. ¹²And he was with them hid in the house of God six years: and Athaliah reigned over the land.

Jehoshabeath, the sister of King Ahaziah, hid Joash from Athaliah, his grandmother, to save his life. She hid him in a room and assigned someone to nurse him up for six years. Joash must have been one year old when he was given to the nurse. He was seven years old when he was made the king of Judah after being nursed for six years. Picture the scenario, a nurse was paid wages to raise the son of a king. Do you think she would dare to discipline or even rebuke him for fear? No, I don't think so, she would not want to lose her job or risk getting punished. She only performed her duties as a nurse and not as a mother. She did not train King Joash; he was a child left to himself.

Proverbs 29:15

The rod and reproof give wisdom: but a child left to himself bringeth his mother to shame.

A child left to himself does not mean that there was no adult in his life. It means that the rod of correction and reproof was not employed in his or her upbringing. The child was not disciplined promptly with the rod of correction, and reproofed for his wrongdoings. King Joash's foundational years were spent feeding him and ensuring he was healthy and happy. He had no godly parent to train him in the way of the LORD, like the case of King Josiah. How did this later affect him adversely? He deviated from following the LORD at his later age after all the godly training he received from Jehoiada the priest. He could only follow the LORD and do right while Jehoiada was alive. But as soon as Jehoiada died, he destroyed all the godly structures that Jehoiada had erected on his life's faulty foundation. He then started to build evil structures that fit the foundation that was laid in his life by Satan.

2Chronicles 24:2, 17-22

2And Joash did that which was right in the sight of the LORD all the days of Jehoiada the priest. 17Now after the death of Jehoiada came the princes of Judah, and made obeisance to the king. Then the king hearkened unto them. 18And they left the house of the LORD God of their fathers, and served groves and idols: and wrath came upon Judah and Jerusalem for this their trespass. 19Yet he sent prophets to them, to bring them again unto the LORD; and they testified against them: but they would not give ear. 20And the Spirit of God came upon Zechariah the son of Jehoiada the priest, which stood above the people, and said unto them, Thus saith God, Why transgress ye the commandments of the LORD, that ye cannot prosper? because ye have forsaken the LORD, he hath also forsaken you. 21And they conspired against him, and stoned him with stones at the commandment of the king in the court of the house of the LORD. 22Thus Joash the king remembered not the kindness which Jehoiada his father had done to him, but

slew his son. And when he died, he said, The LORD look upon it, and require it.

This is why the LORD said in Psalms 11:3, *"If the foundations be destroyed, what can the righteous do?"* All the efforts made by Jehoiada the priest to raise King Joash, a godly man, were in vain. King Joash's foundation was marred and corrupted by Satan because he was a child left to himself. The rod of correction and reproof was not employed in his childhood upbringing. He was not disciplined promptly with the rod of correction, and reproofed for his wrongdoings. Satan used the nurse assigned to Joash to kiddify him. The death-giving goat-like spirit of stubbornness and rebellion filled the void left in his life due to the lack of godly training. Therefore, as soon as Jehoiada died, he rebelled and turned aside to align himself with the foundation that Satan laid in his life.

Sadly, this is the case for many children, especially those in the Western world and of rich parents, no matter their geographic location. These parents neglect the foundational stage of their children's upbringing because they are too busy chasing after wealth, power, and fame, or simply because they are ignorant. They employ nannies and daycares, pay them their wages to waste and lay whatever foundation they deem fit in their children's lives, just like in the case of King Joash.

These parents often devote time to ensure their children get the best nourishment and comfort in life. They take them to the best restaurant to eat, buy them the best electronic gadgets, and provide them luxury bedrooms furnished with TVs and computers. They take them to the best hospitals and ensure regular checkups and good food supplements. They send them to the best schools and employ private lesson teachers. They take them to the best resorts around the world for vacations to ensure they enjoy all the good pleasures of life and are happy.

Christian parents should never raise their children like this. Children raised by nannies and daycares are usually children left to themselves. They will never grow up with the godly foundation of their parents if they have any. The nannies and daycares are only there for their wages, and Satan will use them to lay an ungodly foundation in the lives of your children. Some of these nannies and daycares are Satan's kiddifying agents. Some of these nannies and daycares might be witches and witchhouses. They will surely get your children Kiddified. Christian parents should emulate Jedidah King Josiah's mother, Timothy's grandmother Lois, and mother Eunice in early childhood upbringing. They sacrificed time and resources to labor in training and prayers to raise godly children. Your sacrifices, labor, and prayers will never be in vain, because the Almighty God watches over His Word to perform it, and He said, ***"Train up a child in the way he should go: and when he is old, he will not depart from it."*** Proverbs 22:6. Your sincere godly efforts and sacrifices in early childhood training will eventually bless your life, your family, and humanity. Their lives will bless generations to come just like those of King Josiah and Pastor Timothy, because God watches over His Word to perform it.

2.5: Ground-Zero Godly Training Shields from Peer Pressure and Bad Role Model Influence

There may be no established protection strategies for parents to protect their children from external influences, peer pressure pollution, and negative role models. Nevertheless, when children are given proper godly training from Ground-Zero, it will shield them from all external negative influences. When a solid godly foundation is laid within the foundational character molding years of ages zero to seven. It will form a formidable shield to protect and keep that child from peer pressure and the influence of all negative role models. A good biblical example is that of the child Samuel.

1Samuel 1:20-22

20Wherefore it came to pass, when the time was come about after Hannah had conceived, that she bare a son, and called his name Samuel, saying, Because I have asked him of the LORD 21And the man Elkanah, and all his house, went up to offer unto the LORD the yearly sacrifice, and his vow. 22But Hannah went not up; for she said unto her husband, I will not go up until the child be weaned, and then I will bring him, that he may appear before the LORD, and there abide for ever.

Hannah, being barren, earnestly sought the Lord in prayers for a male child and promised to give the child back to God. God answered her prayers, and she gave birth to Samuel, who became a great prophet in Israel. After the birth of Samuel, Hannah said to her husband that she would not take the child to the house of God until he was weaned. 1Samuel 1:22 **"But Hannah went not up; for she said unto her husband, I will not go up until the child be weaned, and then I will bring him, that he may appear before the LORD, and there abide for ever."** She wanted to wean the child, knowing that he would not be coming back home again once he got there. Weaning means to cause a child to cease elementary dependency on the mother for breast milk and Activities of Daily Living (ADLs), and to cease childish habits. In other words, this means to train up a child. Hannah knew that she needed to perform her duty of training up her child before giving him to the LORD as she promised.

Hannah did not just wean Samuel from dependency on breast milk and Activities for Daily Living (ADLs) but weaned him from the dependency on carnal food. She fed him with spiritual food – the Word of God and taught him to depend on spiritual food. Luke 4:4 ***"And Jesus answered him, saying, it is written, That man shall not live by bread alone, but by every word of God."*** This was what Hannah taught her child, Samuel. She trained him to depend on the Word of God. The age at which Samuel was brought to the House of God and handed over to Eli the priest was not specified. All that is known is that he was brought to the House of the LORD after he was weaned. The right age for weaning in humans ends around seven years. This is evidenced in the Bible with King Josiah and King Joash. They were not made kings until they were weaned. Therefore, one can safely say that Samuel was brought to the house of the Lord at a young age between seven and eight. 1Samuel 1:24. ***"And when she had weaned him, she took him up with her, with three bullocks, and one ephah of flour, and a bottle of wine, and brought him unto the house of the LORD in Shiloh: and the child was young."***

The second aspect of weaning a child is to train the child to cease childish habits. 1Corinthians 13:11, ***"When I was a child, I spake as a child, I understood as a child, I thought as a child: but when I became a man, I put away childish things."*** Childish characters are ungodly because man is born in a sinful state inherited from Adam. That is why you do not have to teach a child how to lie, steal, be greedy, selfish, and manipulate with crying to have his way, etc. The child's natural inclination is to be disorderly, and sinful, and to love the world and the things of the world. 1John 2: 15-16, **"Love not the world, neither the things that are in the world. If any man love the world, the love of the Father is not in him. For all that is in the world, the lust of the flesh, and the lust of the eyes, and the pride of life, is not of the Father, but is of the world."** It takes training to teach a child decorum and to get him to fear and love God. Hannah knew that a child left to himself (without training) would cause grief. Proverbs 29:15, **"The rod and reproof give wisdom: but a child left to himself bringeth his mother to shame."** She did not want to give the LORD a child that would cause shame. She sacrificed all that was necessary to train up a godly child. She denied herself traveling with her husband to the House of the LORD to devote time to raising a godly child for the LORD. King David said he would not give God that which cost him nothing, 2Samuel 24:24. You cannot raise a godly child for the LORD without paying the price for it. Hannah paid the price, and she succeeded. The solid godly foundation she laid in Samuel within the foundational stage (character molding ages, 0 –7) paid off in preserving him from the external influence of peer pressure and ungodly role models.

1Ssamuel 2:12,17,18,22

¹²Now the sons of Eli were sons of Belial; they knew not the LORD. ¹⁷Wherefore the sin of the young men was very great before the LORD: for men abhorred the offering of the LORD. ¹⁸But Samuel ministered before the LORD, being a child, girded with a linen ephod. ²²Now Eli was very old,

and heard all that his sons did unto all Israel; and how they lay with the women that assembled at the door of the tabernacle of the congregation.

Samuel did not learn to fear and love God in Eli's house because Eli and his wife failed to raise godly children for the LORD. They could not train their children in the fear of God. Obviously, they could not have been the ones responsible for the godly outcome of Samuel's life. The fear and the love of God in Samuel were imparted to him at home by his mother, Hannah. Eli the priest and his wife failed God in their duty of raising godly children for the LORD. They could not sacrifice time and resources to train up their children in the fear of God, and they were severely judged and punished by God, 1Samuel 2:27-36. The Bible says that his sons were the sons of Belial, that is, sons of Satan. They did not know God and were evil in their character. They were greedy and sexually immoral, and these were the people with whom Samuel lived in the same house as he grew up. They were Samuel's peers and role models, being his seniors. Yet they could not corrupt him, because his mother laid a solid godly foundation in him at Ground-Zero.

Who else would have had the greatest influence on a young man growing up besides his peers and elder brothers, who are often his immediate role models? Eli's sons were elder brothers and immediate role models for Samuel; he did not follow their evil ways despite being far away from his mother. Satan knew that God had called Samuel to be a great prophet in Israel to restore Justice and righteousness. One could only imagine the peer pressure and temptations that Satan would have daily hurled at Samuel through Eli's sons and others. Nevertheless, he did not give in to peer pressure and evil influence. This was only possible because his mother had laid a solid godly foundation in his life. The godly training Hannah gave Samuel in his foundational years (ages 0 to 7) shielded him from all external influences of peer pressure and negative role models. Samuel did not depart from the godly training he received from his mother. Proverbs 22:6 ***"Train up a child in the way he should go: and when he is old, he will not depart from it."*** Samuel grew up to become a great prophet in Israel with great honor. He never practiced the injustice, greed, and sexual immorality of Eli's sons. He restored justice and righteousness to the people of God, lived a righteous life, and ended his ministry in righteousness.

1Samuel 12:1-5

¹And Samuel said unto all Israel, Behold, I have hearkened unto your voice in all that ye said unto me, and have made a king over you. ²And now, behold, the king walketh before you: and I am old and grayheaded; and, behold, my sons are with you: and I have walked before you from my childhood unto this day. ³Behold, here I am: witness against me before the LORD, and before his anointed: whose ox have I taken? or whose ass have I taken? or whom have I defrauded? whom have I oppressed? or of whose hand have I received any bribe to blind mine eyes therewith? and I will restore it you. ⁴And they said, Thou hast not defrauded us, nor oppressed us, neither hast thou taken ought of any man's hand. ⁵And he said unto them, The LORD is witness against you, and his anointed is witness this day, that ye have not found ought in my hand. And they answered, He is witness.

This is what foundational (early childhood) godly training can produce in a child's life. Glory to God Almighty who watches over His Word to perform them for those who obey Him. God watched over His Word Proverbs 22:6, ***"Train up a child in the way he should go: and when he is old, he will not depart from it."*** and performed it in Samuel's life for Hannah because she believed it and did her part to train Samuel. God will likewise do the same for you; if only you would believe His Word and do your part to sacrifice all that is needed to train your child in the way of the LORD.

2.6: The Crucial Role of Mothers in Ground-Zero Child Training

Mothers play a critical role in child training; their role is decisive for the outcome of a child's life. The role of mothers in child training determines the future of the child. This is so because the foundational stage in character molding is between ages zero to seven, and at this stage, the child is closest to the mother. Between the ages of zero to seven, the child is dependent on the mother for breast milk and ADLs. The child sees the mother as the primary caregiver and looks up to her for food, ADLs, and training. There are also times when men find themselves in this role because of unfortunate circumstances like the death or illness of the mother, because of divorce, or children out of wedlock. It could also be because of socioeconomic status, where the mother is the breadwinner of the home, which may hinder her from playing her motherly role effectively. It could also be a result of the dysfunctional contemporary world where mothers simply neglect their God-given role in child training. Whatever the case may be, the parent in the motherly role at the character molding stage of ages zero to seven should know that he or she is playing a decisive role in the child's life. This period of a child's life should never be taken for granted. It should not be left in the hands of Satan. Nevertheless, the focus here is on the mother to whom God has naturally assigned this role due to her unique qualities and disposition.

Women are naturally the primary caregivers of the child during the character-molding stage. The infant child from day one depends on the mother for food, warmth, and love, which the child receives from suckling. These essential needs provided by the mother naturally create a bond between the child and the mother on day one. This makes the mother the closest person to the child from day one, and training must begin at Ground-Zero to be most effective and lasting. Early years psychology says, "Give me the child until he is seven and I will make him what you want him to be." This psychology says ages 0 –7 are the formative years of a child, character molding-wise. Everything else we do after ages 0 –7 to mold the character of the child cannot be foundational and may not last. The philosophy is, "The earlier the better." Proverbs 22:6 ***"Train up a child in the way he should go: and when he is old, he will not depart from it."***

Mothers play a unique critical role in child training due to their natural disposition. Their role determines the child's future. This character formative years can be likened to "garbage in, garbage out." You will always receive returns with interest on whatever you put in as training, whether good or bad. If you put in nothing because you are so busy with mundane things. Know that there are no vacuums in life, and this also applies to your children. Satan will help you to ensure that your child is filled with garbage and Kiddified through his various agents. Throughout the Scripture, mothers have shaped their children's future through training, whether for good or for evil.

King Ahaziah: 2Chronicles 22:2-4

²Forty and two years old was Ahaziah when he began to reign, and he reigned one year in Jerusalem. His mother's name also was Athaliah the daughter of Omri. ³He also walked in the ways of the house of Ahab: for his mother was his counsellor to do wickedly. ⁴Wherefore he did evil in the sight of the LORD like the house of Ahab: for they were his counsellors after the death of his father to his destruction.

King Ahaziah became an evil king in Judah who did wickedly against the Lord, and the full credit for the outcome of his life was given to his mother Athaliah. The mother did not suddenly become his counselor after he was crowned king as an adult. His mother being his counselor shows that the mother schooled him in evil right from his character formative years, and now that he is old, he cannot depart from evil. The foundation laid in King Ahaziah's life by his mother at Ground-Zero is evil. Therefore, as the king has nothing else to offer but evil, who then should be his counselor? Those who are experts at doing evil, and who else is more qualified in Judah as an evil expert than Athaliah, his mother? Do you now see why his mother became his counselor? The role of a mother in the outcome of a child's life cannot be overemphasized.

King Amon: 2kings 21:19-22

¹⁹Amon was twenty and two years old when he began to reign, and he reigned two years in Jerusalem. And his mother's name was Meshullemeth, the daughter of Haruz of Jotbah. 20And he did that which was evil in the sight of the LORD, as his father Manasseh did. 21And he walked in all the way that his father walked in, and served the idols that his father served, and worshipped them: 22And he forsook the LORD God of his fathers, and walked not in the way of the LORD.

King Amon reigned as an evil king, and his mother is mentioned for us to know who trained him. We must remember that God does not use words carelessly when studying the Scripture. Every word mentioned in the Bible is of great necessity to understanding the message and what took place. Amon's father was King Manasseh, who also did evil in the sight of God and was also trained by his mother Hephzibah. 2Kings 21:1-2,18 *"1Manasseh was twelve years old when he began to reign, and reigned fifty and five years in Jerusalem. And his mother's name was Hephzibah. 2And he did that which was evil in the sight of the LORD, after the abominations of the heathen, whom the LORD cast out before the children of Israel. 18And Manasseh slept with his fathers, and was buried in the garden of his own house, in the garden of Uzza: and Amon his son reigned in his stead."*

Amon's father was a king and obviously would not have the time to provide nursing care and ground-zero training for his son. Moreover, in those days, it was traditional for women to play their natural role in early childhood care and training. He walked in all the ways of his father, does not mean that his father laid that foundation. 2Kings 2:20-21 *"And he did that which was evil in the sight of the LORD, as his father Manasseh did. And he walked in all the way that his father walked in, and served the idols that his father served, and worshipped them:"* Most likely King Manasseh would not have had time to spend with Amon at his foundational stage, ages 0-7. It just shows that his father was also an evil king, and he chose to follow his father's ways. King Amon's outcome in life may have been different if he had a godly mother who laid a godly foundation in his life. This truth can be seen in the case of King Josiah, his son, who had a godly mother who laid a godly foundation in her son's life.

King Josiah: 2Kings 22:1-2

¹Josiah was eight years old when he began to reign, and he reigned thirty and one years in Jerusalem. And his mother's name was Jedidah, the daughter of Adaiah of Boscath. ²And he did that which was right in the sight of the LORD, and walked in all the way of David his father, and turned not aside to the right hand or to the left.

Josiah became king at age eight and did that which was right in the sight of the Lord all the days of his life. Amazingly, King Amon, who did evil like his father King Manasseh, was the father of King Josiah. Nonetheless, King Josiah did not turn out to do evil like his father, King Amon. Rather, he walked in the way of his father David. King David is King Josiah's grandfather of many generations. King Josiah never knew King David in person, it was just to show that King Josiah chose to walk in the ways of King David, as seen in the case of King Amon, who chose to walk in the way of his father King Manasseh. The outcome of King Josiah's life was different from that of his father, King Amon, though they both had evil fathers. The godly outcome of King Josiah's life was different because he had a godly mother who did a great job in training him to become a godly child like his father, David. The Ground-Zero godly child training his mother, Jedidah laid formed the bedrock of King Josiah's character. This godly foundation enabled King Josiah to choose to do that which was right in the sight of the LORD all the days of his life. King Josaiah's mother's role in his Ground-Zero training, that is, early childhood training, is clearly revealed in 2Kings 22:1, *"Josiah was eight years old when he began to reign, and he reigned thirty and one years in Jerusalem. And his mother's name was Jedidah, the daughter of Adaiah of Boscath."* Again, we can clearly see that the outcome of King Josiah's life was fully credited to his mother. "Give me the child until he is seven and I will make him what you want him to be." Who was with Josiah from ages zero to seven? His mother Jedidah. She did not fail in her duty, and the Word of God came true for her. Proverbs 22:6 *"Train up a child in the way he should go: and when he is old, he will not depart from it."* Many mothers failed to adequately play this critical role in their children's lives, and when the inevitable ungodly outcome begins to manifest, then they start to fast and pray. This is not to say that you should not fast and pray in such a situation. But, sacrificing time and resources to train your child, especially in their foundational stage of ages 0 – 7, is far more important, effective, and rewarding than any corrective measure one may take in the future.

King Jehoahaz 2Kings 23:29-32

29In his days Pharaohnechoh king of Egypt went up against the king of Assyria to the river Euphrates: and king Josiah went against him; and he slew him at Megiddo, when he had seen him. 30And his servants carried him in a chariot dead from Megiddo, and brought him to Jerusalem, and buried him in his own sepulchre. And the people of the land took Jehoahaz the son of Josiah, and anointed him, and made him king in his father's stead. ³¹Jehoahaz was twenty and three years old when he began to reign; and he reigned three months in Jerusalem. And his mother's name was Hamutal, the daughter of Jeremiah of Libnah. ³²And he did that which was evil in the sight of the LORD, according to all that his fathers had done.

King Jehoahaz was the son of King Josiah, a godly man who served God faithfully all the days of his life. How then did his son turn out to be an evil person? It is crucial to pay good attention to this storyline. King Josiah had an evil father, King Amon, yet he did not turn out to be an evil person. On the other hand, King Josiah's son, King Jehoahaz, turned out to be evil despite having a father as godly as King Josiah. Jehoahaz became evil because he had a mother who did not sacrifice time and pleasure to train him in the way of the LORD at his foundational stage. His mother, Hamutal, was mentioned to inform us of the person responsible for his upbringing during his foundational stage of age zero to seven. King Josiah turned out to be a godly person despite having an evil father, King Amon. This was possible because of a godly mother who sacrificed time and pleasure to train him in the way of the LORD at his foundational stage. Mothers play a critical and decisive role in the outcome of a child's character. The role of mothers in child training determines the character of the child. This is so because the child is closest to the mother and dependent on her for everything at the foundational stage in character molding. What mothers do or fail to do to mold the child's character at this stage will ultimately decide whether the child will become good or evil.

King Lemuel: Proverbs 31:1-5

¹The words of king Lemuel, the prophecy that his mother taught him. ²What, my son? and what, the son of my womb? and what, the son of my vows? ³Give not thy strength unto women, nor thy ways to that which destroyeth kings. ⁴It is not for kings, O Lemuel, it is not for kings to drink wine; nor for princes strong drink: ⁵Lest they drink, and forget the law, and pervert the judgment of any of the afflicted.

These are the words of King Lemuel. Obviously, he was a good king as reflected in his words in Proverbs Chapter 31. Who taught him to do right as revealed in the Scripture? his mother. Proverbs 31:1 **"The words of King Lemuel, the prophecy that his mother taught him."** The full credit for the outcome of King Lemuel's life was again given to his mother. His mother taught him that women, wine, and strong drinks destroy destiny. She sang it like a song to Lemuel until it was engraved on the foundation of his life. He did not depart from his mother's teachings because they were laid at the foundational stage of his life. The life and words of King Lemuel, as taught to him by his mother, are still blessing humanity today. Proverbs 22:6 *"Train up a child in the way he should go: and when he is old, he will not depart from it."*

Prophet Samuel: 1Samuel 1:20-22; 12:1,3-5

²²But Hannah went not up; for she said unto her husband, I will not go up until the child be weaned, and then I will bring him, that he may appear before the LORD, and there abide for ever. ¹And Samuel said unto all Israel, Behold, I have hearkened unto your voice in all that ye said unto me, and have made a king over you. ³Behold, here I am: witness against me before the LORD, and before his anointed: whose ox have I taken? or whose ass have I taken? or whom have I defrauded? whom have I oppressed? or of whose hand have I received any bribe to blind mine eyes therewith? and I will restore it you. ⁴And they said, Thou hast not defrauded us, nor oppressed us, neither hast thou taken ought of any man's hand. ⁵And he said unto them, The LORD is witness against you, and his anointed is witness this day, that ye have not found ought in my hand. And they answered, He is witness.

Prophet Samuel's mother, Hannah, sacrificed time, resources, and pleasure to train Samuel to be a godly child. The fear and the love of God in Samuel were imparted to him at home by his mother, Hannah, during his foundational stage of ages 0 – 7. She said I will not go up until the child is weaned. This means to train a child to cease elementary dependency on the mother for breast milk and Activities of Daily Living (ADLs), and to cease childish habits. Hannah knew that she needed to perform her duty of training up her child before giving him to the LORD as she promised. 1Samuel 1:22, *"But Hannah went not up; for she said unto her husband, I will not go up until the child be weaned, and then I will bring him, that he may appear before the LORD, and there abide for ever."* She denied herself travel, even to the house of God, just to devote time to training her son. She understood the importance of early childhood training. She knew that it would form the bedrock of Samuel's life. Because of this, she was willing to sacrifice whatever it would take to lay a solid godly foundation for her son. In contrast, many Christian women in contemporary times will not sacrifice vacation, pleasure, work, time, and resources to raise a godly child for the LORD. Yet they wonder why their children are manifesting ungodly characters. Some go as far as blaming and questioning God. Look inward instead, look at the mirror, and ask the woman in the mirror; Did you really do your job as a mother in training up that child? Ask yourself, am I really doing my job right now as a mother in training up my child? Ask yourself, have I really sacrificed all that is necessary to raise a godly child for the LORD? You will not reap what you have not sown.

Hannah reaped the fruits of her labor. Samuel did not bring her shame but honor as it is today. Prophet Samuel did not depart from the path he was trained to follow all the days of his life. Evil was not found in him by God and by man; he did that which was right in the sight of God all through his ministry. Here is the conversation between Prophet Samuel and the children of Israel at the end of his ministry *"Behold, here I am: witness against me before the LORD, and before his anointed: whose ox have I taken? or whose ass have I taken? or whom have I defrauded? whom have I oppressed? or of whose hand have I received any bribe to blind mine eyes therewith? and I will restore it you. And they said, Thou hast not defrauded us, nor oppressed us, neither hast thou taken ought of any man's hand. And he said unto them, The LORD is witness against you, and his anointed is witness this day, that ye have not found ought in my hand. And they answered, He is witness."* This is the outcome of sacrificial labor in child training by a godly woman. Hannah honored God by taking heed to obey God's Word, and God honored His Word in her life. Proverbs 22:6 *"Train up a child in the way he should go: and when he is old, he will not depart from it."* The good news is that it is not too late to make amends and do something. Woman! God is counting on you to raise Him godly children. May you find grace to accomplish this as you obey and take actions of faith in Jesus' name, Amen.

Pastor Timothy: 2Timothy 1:5; 3:14-15

1:5When I call to remembrance the unfeigned (genuine) faith that is in thee, which dwelt first in thy grandmother Lois, and thy mother Eunice; and I am persuaded that in thee also. 3:14But continue thou in the things which thou hast learned and hast been assured of, knowing of whom thou hast learned them; 3:15And that from a child thou hast known the holy scriptures, which are able to make thee wise unto salvation through faith which is in Christ Jesus.

The genuine faith and godly character Apostle Paul witnessed in the life of Pastor Timothy were imparted to him in his childhood by his mother and grandmother. 2Timothy 3:15 ***"And that from a child thou hast known the holy scriptures, which are able to make thee wise unto salvation through faith which is in Christ Jesus."*** Why were Timothy's grandfather and father not credited for his godly life? It is because his godly character was imparted to him when he was a child at the foundational stage of ages 0 – 7; his mother and grandmother were the ones who weaned him. Naturally, as God has ordained it, and also traditionally, a child is more attached to his mother for loving care, food, and warmth at this stage. Timothy's mother and grandmother did not waste his precious character-molding stage by pampering him and spoiling him with grandma's love. They sacrificed all that was necessary to raise a godly child for the LORD. Glory to God Almighty for a godly and disciplined grandmother who did not spoil her grandchild with ungodly love, but dedicated time to training him in the fear of the LORD. It is also evident that it was Lois, Timothy's grandmother, who trained up Eunice, his mother, to become the godly woman who also trained up a godly child for the LORD.

Mothers always receive credit and acknowledgement for a well-trained, godly child, as seen in the Scripture. God and man will always praise the mother for a godly child because mothers are naturally disposed to train the child within the character-formative years. Consequently, the mother will always receive the blame from both God and man for an ungodly child. When King Saul thought that his son Jonathan was behaving foolishly. He quickly turned his anger on Jonathan's mother because he believed she had raised an unreasonable child for him.

Proverbs 10:1

The proverbs of Solomon. A wise son maketh a glad father: but a foolish son is the heaviness of his mother.

1 Samuel 20:30

Then Saul's anger was kindled against Jonathan, and he said unto him, Thou son of the perverse rebellious woman, do not I know that thou hast chosen the son of Jesse to thine own confusion, and unto the confusion of thy mother's nakedness?

The role of a mother in raising godly children for the LORD cannot be overemphasized. Ages zero to seven are the most important and effective period in child training, character molding-wise. The impact of character training done at this stage is life-changing and life-lasting. At this stage, the child is not yet rigid, but tender and easy to mold. Women are naturally and traditionally positioned to exploit this opportunity. Failure to do so leaves a vacuum for Satan and his agents to exploit and kiddify the child. That is, turn them into untrained, stubborn, and rebellious goat-like spirited hell-bound children of Satan. Mothers and grandmothers, please make the best use of this period to raise godly children for the LORD. God is counting on you. Honor God by taking heed to obey His Word in training up your child early, and God will honor His Word in your life and your family by keeping that child in His way all the days of his life. Proverbs 22:6, *"Train up a child in the way he should go: and when he is old, he will not depart from*

CHAPTER 3

Invest Time and Resources in Training

Time is a highly valued asset, and all you are today are the results of all the time and resources you invested in the past. Whether it is your education, finances, job, and so on, they are the proceeds, or the value of the time and resources you invested. Whatever is worth our time automatically attracts our material and intellectual resources. That is why some people are paid according to their time, that is, hourly wages. Two people with the same qualifications can work in the same company but not receive the same paycheck amount because one of them works overtime. The more the hours, the more the pay. In the same way, the more hours you invest in godly training for your children, the greater will be your paychecks (rewards).

You went to school, you invested hours of studies and financial resources, and that is why you came out with a degree. Your certificate is a product of the time and resources you invested. When we invest time and resources, we reap rewards. Then why are you not investing enough time and resources in your children, and you are expecting rewards?

3.1 Children Are Your Only Assets of Eternal Value

Training requires the investment of time and resources to acquire the desired results. Your teachers who trained you in school invested time and resources in the classroom. The results you achieved may not have been achieved if they had not been there to spend their time and resources. Every asset you have ever acquired in life, be it tangible or intangible, is a product of your time and resource investments. The state of your marriage today is a product of the amount of time and resources you have invested in your marital relationship. Your children are direct products of the time and resources invested in your marriage. They are assets acquired through the investment of your time and resources. Your children are your only assets with eternal value. Should they not get the most out of your resources and time investments?

Job 1:1-3

¹There was a man in the land of Uz, whose name was Job; and that man was perfect and upright, and one that feared God, and eschewed evil. ²And there were born unto him seven sons and three daughters. ³His substance also was seven thousand sheep, and three thousand camels, and five hundred yoke of oxen, and five hundred she asses, and a very great household; so that this man was the greatest of all the men of the east.

Job 42:10, 12-13

¹⁰And the LORD turned the captivity of Job, when he prayed for his friends: also the LORD gave Job twice as much as he had before. ¹²So the LORD blessed the latter end of Job more than his beginning: for he had fourteen thousand

sheep, and six thousand camels, and a thousand yoke of oxen, and a thousand she asses. *13*He had also seven sons and three daughters.

This story about Job clarifies my earlier statement, "Your children are your only assets with eternal value." The Bible clearly states in Job 42:10 that the LORD gave Job twice as much as he had before. But if you look at the last verse above, that is Job 42:13, it says that God gave Job seven sons and three daughters. How come? Job had seven sons and three daughters in the beginning, who all died. If God said He gave Job twice as much as he had before. Should his new children not have been twenty, fourteen sons and six daughters? Or does this mean that the Scripture is inaccurate? Certainly not! Job invested much time and resources in training and preserving his children in holiness.

Job 1:4-5,18-19

4And his sons went and feasted in their houses, every one his day; and sent and called for their three sisters to eat and to drink with them. 5And it was so, when the days of their feasting were gone about, that Job sent and sanctified them, and rose up early in the morning, and offered burnt offerings according to the number of them all: for Job said, it may be that my sons have sinned, and cursed God in their hearts. Thus did Job continually. 18While he was yet speaking, there came also another, and said, Thy sons and thy daughters were eating and drinking wine in their eldest brother's house: 19And, behold, there came a great wind from the wilderness, and smote the four corners of the house, and it fell upon the young men, and they are dead; and I only am escaped alone to tell thee.

Children are assets of eternal value. If quality time and resources are invested to raise them godly, they will last eternally. Job spent much of his time and resources on his children. Job will rise up early in the morning to offer burnt offerings to sanctify his children, not because they have sinned, but just in case they have sinned. He did not take any chances nor spare his time and resources when it came to his children because he knew they were his most valuable assets. The Bible states that "Thus did Job continually." Job was consistent in sacrificing time and resources to ensure that his children were holy before God. Job's ten children were not lost; they only changed their dwelling place through death. The ten of them were in Paradise waiting for Job. That was why God only gave him back ten children. The first ten were not lost; they only changed location. When Job died, he was reunited with the first ten children, and when the last ten died, they were reunited with Job. The Word of God is accurate, the LORD gave Job twice as much as he had before, including children.

All other assets you have acquired with time and resources, like your money, house, etc., will all perish in this world. Job understood this and invested more time and resources in raising godly children. The only assets he retained from this world when he died were his children. Your children are your only assets with the potential of eternal value. If you train up godly children, they will make heaven, and you will be with them forever if you make heaven. Parents should ensure to work together to raise godly children for the LORD. Children are your most valuable assets with eternal value. Therefore, invest enough of your time and resources to ensure that they are trained in the way of the LORD.

3.2 Investing Time and Resources Require Sacrifice

Jedidah, King Josiah's mother, did not succeed in raising such a godly son by running from pillar to post for jobs and extra hours. Investing adequate time and resources in a child from zero to seven years requires sacrifices. It may require quitting your job. The third strategy of Satan, according to the Satanic Ten Points Agenda, is to destroy the Judeo-Christian family structure. That is the traditional Christian family structure. This is why we see wives competing with their husbands instead of complementing them; it is a Satanic strategy at work. The wife wants to earn more than her husband. Instead of submitting to her husband and staying home to train and raise godly children, she dumps them in daycare in pursuit of dollars.

I am not saying that wives should not work. I am simply saying that husband and wife should work together in harmony, following biblical order to raise godly children for the LORD. According to God's word, husband and wife are one and not two individualistically driven people. Genesis 2:24, ***"Therefore shall a man leave his father and his mother, and shall cleave unto his wife: and they shall be one flesh."*** The wife should never neglect her primary role of ensuring that a solid godly foundation is laid in the lives of the children in their foundational stage of ages zero to seven. The Bible says that the desire of the woman shall be for her husband. This means that once a woman gets married, her desires should be aligned with her husband's desires. Once a woman is married, there is no more room for individualistic pursuits or aspirations. God expects her to complement her husband's pursuits and aspirations as one flesh.

Genesis 3:16

Unto the woman he (God) said, I will greatly multiply thy sorrow and thy conception; in sorrow thou shalt bring forth children; and thy desire shall be to thy husband, and he shall rule over thee.

Submission of the wife to her husband in obedience to God's Word is absolutely necessary in achieving the goal of raising godly children. Raising godly children will never be possible if two captains are in the family boat or two opposing competitors. If the wife understands that it takes time to train godly children, and that she is one with her husband. She will quit her job where necessary or reduce her work hours to ensure she is available to train their children, especially within the ages of zero to seven.

However, what is commonly seen these days is mothers throwing their children into one daycare or another or handing them over to nannies. Then they are the first to cry, "I don't know why this child is behaving like this. This kind of thing has never happened in our family, I don't know where he learned it from. God, why?" Do you honestly don't know? You took the child from one witch house (daycare) to another, from one nanny to another. And you are wondering where he learned the strange behaviors you are seeing? If need be, quit your job or reduce your work hours so that you can invest time in training your children, especially when they are in their foundational stage, which is their formative years of character molding.

Parents should lay a godly foundation in their children on which they and others can build upon. Timothy's grandmother and mother laid a godly foundation in him on which Apostle Paul built upon. Which foundation are you laying in your children for others to build upon? Children spend very little time with their parents once they start schooling. The little time that parents have should be spent on investing godly values into them. Parents should not just spend time pouring in values but also sifting and draining out all the junk they gather from school. Raising godly children will require much sacrifice to be able to provide the time and resources needed.

Unfortunately, some parents are very busy making money or building careers. Wives, if your husbands do not spend time with the children, you should. Again, remember that Jedidah, King Josiah's mother, was the parent behind King Josiah's godliness. This is what the Bible says about King Josiah's father, King Amon:

2Kings 21:19-22

[19]Amon was twenty and two years old when he began to reign, and he reigned two years in Jerusalem. And his mother's name was Meshullemeth, the daughter of Haruz of Jotbah. [20]And he did that which was evil in the sight of the LORD, as his father Manasseh did. [21]And he walked in all the way that his father walked in, and served the idols that his father served, and worshipped them: [22]And he forsook the LORD God of his fathers, and walked not in the way of the LORD.

It is obvious from this Scripture that the ungodly King Amon did not have a hand in his son's godly upbringing. Otherwise, King Josiah would not have turned out to be a godly king because his evil father would have influenced him to also do evil. Young parents should always observe the consequences of not raising godly children in the lives of older folks and learn, so they do not make the same mistake. Those with children within the foundational age of character molding should rise with great zeal and lay a godly foundation in their children. Those who are not married yet or married and yet to have children have better opportunities to prepare to train their children in the way of the LORD.

Some parents run around trying to make ends meet financially because they failed to plan well in their days of singlehood. Instead of planning and saving for their future, they were busy spending their future, buying cars of various brands, shoes and clothes, and big houses to show off. Seek counsel, and lay a good financial foundation that can help you when you get married and start having children. Instead of buying a personal home first, buy a rental income property. You can buy a four-unit house and rent out three apartments. In that way, you may never have any problem with rent or mortgage again. This will allow you to stay home to train your children and still earn income without working.

As a single adult, you can buy a four-family unit house, work hard to pay it off, or aggressively pay extra money to reduce the principal in the first year of the mortgage. This will save you much on interest and shorten the time needed to pay off the mortgage. As a single, you have all the time to work hard, don't just work hard, work harder, and do not waste your singlehood on frivolities. You need to plan for marriage and family life while single; failure to plan is simply planning to fail. If you plan well and work hard at it, by the time you marry and start having children. You would have gotten an income property that will bring you sweat-free money and give you the financial leverage to spend less time working and more time training your children.

Training children requires time, sacrifice everything necessary to create time, be it your youthful pleasure or your job as needed. Children are the most valuable asset in life with eternal value; if you raise them godly. Sacrifice all it takes to create time for their godly training, and great shall be your reward.

CHAPTER 4

Call Them Children and Not Kids

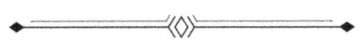

Many parents have ignorantly Kiddified their children. A Kiddified child is an untrained child who has been turned into a spiritual goat and dedicated to Satan. There are many ways in which parents kiddify their children. One of which is by calling their children kids. Many people in contemporary times, especially in the Western world, call children "kids". The media, movies, and songs echo this. It is acceptable across all spheres of life to call children kids. The secular world, the church, and parents are all on board in calling children kids. Most people and parents in the Western world call children "kids" except for a few with understanding. In actuality, a kid is a young goat, and many have no idea that a kid is the name for a young goat. Nonetheless, does it really matter what names we call the children? Is calling the children kids (goats) just a harmless nomenclature? Would a careful biblical examination of calling children kids lead us to the conclusion that it is a harmless nomenclature? Have your children been Kiddified? Let us carefully examine the pages of the Scripture and see what it says on this subject matter.

4.1: The Power of Spoken Words

Words are powerful and capable of altering the speaker's life and those of the hearers. The words that proceed from a person's mouth will reveal his or her person. Your words are your personhood, and you cannot be separated from your words. You are the same person with your spoken or written words. This is why you could get sued or even killed for the words you spoke or wrote, because your word is you and you will be held accountable for your words.

Matthew 12:36-37

36But I say unto you, that every idle word that men shall speak, they shall give account thereof in the day of judgment. 37For by thy words thou shalt be justified, and by thy words thou shalt be condemned.

John 1:1-3,14

1In the beginning was the Word, and the Word was with God, and the Word was God. 2The same was in the beginning with God. 3All things were made by him; and without him was not anything made that was made. 14And the Word was made flesh, and dwelt among us, (and we beheld his glory, the glory as of the only begotten of the Father,) full of grace and truth.

John 3:1-3 clearly reveals that a person is not different from his or her word. The passage shows that God is the same as His Word. The Scripture personifies the Word of God. It says that all things were made by the Word of God, and that the Word of God is God. This means that the words that proceeded from the mouth of God in the beginning to create all things was the same as God, which is Jesus Christ, the Word made flesh.

Genesis 1:1-3;31

1In the beginning God created the heaven and the earth. 2And the earth was without form, and void; and darkness was upon the face of the deep. And the Spirit of God moved upon the face of the waters. ³And God said, let there be light: and there was light. ³¹And God saw everything that he had made, and, behold, it was very good. And the evening and the morning were the sixth day.

Words are spiritual and very powerful, and could be used to create or destroy life. The creation account (Genesis 1:1-31) reveals that God spoke everything into existence by the Words of His mouth, which is also Him. This gives us a glimpse of the power of the spoken word. This is not particular to God alone, it also pertains to humans because God created man in His own image and likeness.

Genesis 1:26-27

²⁶And God said, let us make man in our image, after our likeness: and let them have dominion over the fish of the sea, and over the fowl of the air, and over the cattle, and over all the earth, and over every creeping thing that creepeth upon the earth. ²⁷So God created man in his own image, in the image of God created he him; male and female created he them.

Throughout the Scripture are numerous examples of men of God exercising the power of the spoken word to speak life or destruction into existence. The Bible made it known to mankind that the power of life and death is in the tongue. Proverbs 18:21, *"Death and life are in the power of the tongue: and they that love it shall eat the fruit thereof."* One good example of this as it relates to children is the story of Prophet Elisha and the children of the city.

2Kings 2:25-24

²³And he went up from thence unto Bethel: and as he was going up by the way, there came forth little children out of the city, and mocked him, and said unto him, go up, thou bald head; go up, thou bald head. ²⁴And he turned back, and looked on them, and cursed them in the name of the LORD. And there came forth two she bears out of the wood, and tare forty and two children of them.

It was only at Prophet Elisha's spoken word that these bears came out of the wood and destroyed these 42 children. This is why parents must be very careful in cursing or name-calling their children. Permit me to tell you a true story about a daughter and her mother. It happened that the daughter was obstinate and would not obey or respect the mother at all times. So, a day came that she put up one of her obstinate behaviors which I may not remember exactly now but out of provocations the mother laid a curse on her by saying these words; " for this thing you have done, you will suffer before you give birth to any child, you will suffer so as to know the pains I went through to have you and you have the right to this". It was just casual, but the power in her spoken words resonated years later, after the daughter got married, while in the labor room. The story had it that this young lady labored for days, and while in the hospital, pastors were invited to come and pray for her, but to no avail. The doctors were confused as to why the baby wouldn't come out despite the full dilation and smooth process. The Holy Spirit reminded her of her mother's words years back, and she requested that her mother be sought for immediately. People were asking what her mother would do in a situation like this when she is not a medical professional. As soon as the mother arrived, the daughter began to ask for forgiveness, but the mother was ignorant of the past ordeal as the daughter narrated. However, she queued in immediately and began to reverse all her spoken words following her daughter's confession. While she was broken and still speaking with deep emotions, the baby came forth, and people became speechless while learning their lesson. Just imagine that the mother was no more; what do you think would have happened? Probably she would have died or lost the child.

In the same line was a story of a man in my village whose father cursed him for raising his hand against him. The father cursed him out of annoyance, the father said, "For this act, you shall never set your eyes on me again." As the son returned to his base in Cameroon, he died and never set his eyes on his father again. Words are powerful tools that must be used wisely by parents. Therefore, parents who want to raise godly children for the LORD must desist from cursing their children. They must be very discerning and understand the meaning and spiritual implications of every word they use on their children. Words are spirit and can bring about life or death. John 6:63, ***"It is the spirit that quickeneth; the flesh profiteth nothing: the words that I speak unto you, they are spirit, and they are life."*** Jesus said that the words he speaks are spirit and life. The opposite side of this will be that the words that Satan speaks are spirit, and they are death. Therefore, when someone speaks, the words spoken, if inspired by Jesus they will be releasing a life-giving spirit. Also, when someone speaks words inspired by Satan, he or she will be uttering and releasing a death-giving spirit. One of the words frivolously used by parents on their children in contemporary times is "kid". In actuality, kid means young goat, and your child is not a goat. If calling children kids is inspired by Satan, then we can be certain that it is not just a harmless nomenclature. We can be certain that it invokes the spirit of stubbornness and rebellion in the children – the death-giving spirit.

Genesis 37:31, And they took Joseph's coat, and killed a kid of the goats, and dipped the coat in the blood;

Genesis 38:17, And he said, I will send thee a kid from the flock. And she said, wilt thou give me a pledge, till thou send it?

Numbers 7:16, One kid of the goats for a sin offering:

Isaiah 11:6, The wolf also shall dwell with the lamb, and the leopard shall lie down with the kid; and the calf and the young lion and the fatling together; and a little child shall lead them.

Above are just a few Scriptures that tell us what a kid is in the Bible. The dictionary also made it clear that a kid is a young goat. Isaiah 11:6 talks about the future millennial reign of Jesus Christ and the peace and safety that would be attained. How wild and ferocious beasts such as wolves, leopards, and lions would live in peace with domestic animals like lamb, kid, and calf, and a little child will take care of them. This verse clearly shows that the creator made a clear distinction between a kid and a child. God calls human offspring children, and not kids (goats). Proverbs 22:6 says, Train up your CHILD, not your KID (GOAT). Why do you call them goats and expect them to behave like children? The question you should ask is, why did the world invent the idea of calling children "kids" and why not lambs? It is because God called His own Lamb, and Satan must create the opposite. John 1:36, *"And looking upon Jesus as he walked, he saith, Behold the Lamb of God!"*

This clearly reveals the mastermind behind this kid-calling invention. It is in the DNA of Satan to try to change whatever God says and does to the very opposite; to call good evil and evil good. God created two genders, male and female. Satan and his agents are saying that there are multiplicities of genders, and you can change your gender to any imaginary gender of your choice from hell. They also deny that man was created by God in His own image. They claim that man evolved from other animals, which had their long evolutionary journey from rocks after a big bang that took place billions of years ago. It is Satan's character to try to change whatever God says to the very opposite. Satan is the mastermind behind calling good, evil, and evil, good. God called the offspring of man, children, and Satan has deceived humanity to change it into goats (kids). Jesus called his children sheep, and Satan has deceived humanity to call their own goats (kids). Is calling children goats (kids) just a harmless nomenclature? If the mastermind behind calling the children goats is Satan, then you can be certain that it is not just a harmless nomenclature. If calling the children kids was inspired by Satan, then you can be sure that it invokes a death-giving spirit in them. Words are spirit and can bring about life or death. John 6:63, *"It is the spirit that quickeneth; the flesh profiteth nothing: the words that I speak unto you, they are spirit, and they are life."* Jesus said that the words he speaks are spirit and life. The opposite side of this will be that the words that Satan speaks are spirit, and they are death. Therefore, when someone speaks words inspired by Satan, he or she will be uttering and releasing a death-giving spirit. A Kid is the Satanic informal way of addressing a child. Therefore, do not turn your children into spiritual goats through your spoken words. If calling children "kids" was inspired by Satan, then they must be releasing a death-giving spirit when uttered. Parents who want to train godly children should desist from calling their children kids. Call them children, and not kids (goats).

4.2: The Effects of Names on Bearers

Someone may ask, does it matter if I call them children or kids (goats)? Have you ever heard of the saying: "If you want to kill a dog, give it a bad name?" Nothing has changed in the dog's character; it is the same good dog. But if you want to kill it, just give it a bad name. That means the name will influence how people see, react, or respond to that dog. If you see a good dog coming and start saying; This mad dog is coming, people will either run or go on the offensive and attack the dog to protect themselves. The dog is not mad, but calling it a mad dog automatically changes how people respond to it. No matter how good a dog is, if you give it a bad name, people will view and relate to it according to that name. This is just one aspect of name-calling.

Have you also heard of this idiom: Great or high-sounding name that kills the little dog? These idioms are not really talking about dogs, but human beings. The idioms are simply saying that you can destroy a person with external or internal forces by the name you call him or her. In the first idiom, the name destroys the bearer from outsiders. People respond or deal with that person based on the influence of what they have heard about the person. In the second case, "great or high-sounding name that kills the little dog," this name affects the dog itself and destroys it from within. The dog is given a high-sounding name that makes it feel it is something greater than it really is. A great or high-sounding name will instill pride in a person and cause him or her to want to carry himself/herself to measure up to that high-sounding name. Some of us grew up answering various kinds of nicknames. For example, Superman, Iron Man, Hulk Hogan, and Spider-Man, to name a few. Did those names not stir us up to want to act like those names' characters? Certainly yes, names are highly influential and affect us from within or from without. In Mark 3:17, Jesus nicknamed James and his brother John "Boanerges," which means The Sons of Thunder, and in Luke 9:51-56, we see them trying to live up to that name.

Mark 3:17

And James the son of Zebedee, and John the brother of James; and he surnamed them Boanerges, which is, The sons of thunder:

Luke 9:51-56

⁵¹And it came to pass, when the time was come that he should be received up, he steadfastly set his face to go to Jerusalem, ⁵²And sent messengers before his face: and they went, and entered into a village of the Samaritans, to make ready for him. ⁵³And they did not receive him, because his face was as though he would go to Jerusalem. ⁵⁴And when his disciples James and John saw this, they said, Lord, wilt thou that we command fire to come down from heaven, and consume them, even as Elias did? ⁵⁵But he turned, and rebuked them, and said, Ye know not what manner of spirit ye are of. ⁵⁶For the Son of man is not come to destroy men's lives, but to save them. And they went to another village.

Satan also understands this principle, and since his goal had always been to eradicate godliness and destroy Christianity. He knew to start from the foundation, our children, and to start with the basics of changing their names. Just like God changed the name of Jacob to Israel. He changed their names from children to goats (kids). Let us look at some of the Satanic Ten-Point Agenda by Alice A. Bailey for the New World Order and understand how the devil has been working in the past years.

1. Take God and prayer out of the education system. If people grow up without reference to God, they will consider God irrelevant to daily life. (In the last fifty years, this has happened. God is irrelevant to most people.)
2. Reduce parental authority over children. Break communication between parents and children so the parents can't pass on spiritual values to their children. Do this by pushing excessive child rights.
3. Destroy the traditional Christian family structure. Break the traditional Judeo-Christian family concept.
4. If sex is free, make abortion legal and easy. Remove restrictions on sex. Sex is the biggest Joy, and Christianity robs people of this. People must be freed to enjoy it without restrictions.

From the few points mentioned above, we can clearly see that the devil's primary target is our children. Most of these plans were implemented more than fifty years ago. Many who were raised within that age group in the Western world don't want anything to do with God, or at best very little to do with Him. This is because they were mostly raised as goats (kids). Goats are stubborn and rebellious; they have the character of witchcraft because rebellion is like the sin of witchcraft. Goats are known

72

for their stubbornness, and many are familiar with the term "Stubborn goat," usually used to describe a stubborn person. The Bible in 1Samuel 15:23 says that **"stubbornness is as iniquity and idolatry."** Stubbornness equates to the sin of idolatry, and the idol worshipped is the father goat- Satan. The spiritual reality is that goats – the Kiddified (Those with goatlike character) have no place in the kingdom of God.

1Samuel 15:23

For rebellion is as the sin of witchcraft, and stubbornness is as iniquity and idolatry. Because thou hast rejected the word of the LORD, he hath also rejected thee from being king.

I emphasize name-calling because it is a significant aspect of child training that parents must consider if they want to succeed in correcting their children's character. Now remember that the point here is not so much the name itself, but the source and purpose for the name. God wants to create a paradigm shift with this knowledge about calling our children goats, in order to realign our thoughts and beliefs with His Word on how we view and deal with our children. The realignment of thought and mind that will cause parents to train their children adequately in the ways of the LORD.

Genesis 32:28

And he said, thy name shall be called no more Jacob, but Israel: for as a prince hast thou power with God and with men, and hast prevailed.

God changed Jacob's name to Israel as seen in the above Scripture. Why did God change Jacob's name? Was it just that Jacob did not sound right, or was there a bigger picture to it?

Certainly, there was a bigger picture to it. Despite changing Jacob's name, when God appeared to Moses in the burning bush centuries later, He still referred to Himself as the God of Abraham, Isaac, and Jacob. Also, when Jesus spoke to the Sadducees on the resurrection of the dead, He referred to God as the God of Abraham, Isaac, and Jacob. Why is God still calling him Jacob despite changing his name to Israel?

Exodus 3:6

Moreover, he said, I am the God of thy father, the God of Abraham, the God of Isaac, and the God of Jacob. And Moses hid his face; for he was afraid to look upon God.

Matthew 22:31-32

[31]But as touching the resurrection of the dead, have ye not read that which was spoken unto you by God, saying, [32]I am the God of Abraham, and the God of Isaac, and the God of Jacob? God is not the God of the dead, but of the living.

Jesus still referred to God as the God of Jacob. Why not the God of Israel? It is because it was not really about the name, but the reprogramming of Jacob's mind to create a paradigm shift in how he views and treats himself and his family. God wanted to achieve a reprogramming of Jacob's mindset to birth a nation. Therefore, from that day onward, Jacob never viewed himself again as just a family, but as one through whom God would raise a nation. The name change created a paradigm shift in Jacob's beliefs, and he saw himself as a nation and not just another family. If the name change, which altered Jacob's view of himself and his family, had not happened. He and his family would have been swallowed up in Egypt, and there would have been no nation called Israel today. They would have all ended up in Egypt, diffused there, and become Egyptians.

But because God had created in them the mindset that they were not just a family, but a nation of their own. They went into Egypt believing they were a nation called Israel and would surely come out of Egypt to their own land. Let us have a glimpse of their transformed mindset in the words of Jacob himself and his son Joseph, as seen below.

Genesis 48:21

And Israel said unto Joseph, Behold, I die: but God shall be with you, and bring you again unto the land of your fathers.

Genesis 50:24-25

24And Joseph said unto his brethren, I die: and God will surely visit you, and bring you out of this land unto the land which he swore to Abraham, to Isaac, and to Jacob. 25And Joseph took an oath of the children of Israel, saying, God will surely visit you, and ye shall carry up my bones from hence.

God visited Jacob and created in him a paradigm shift in belief, which he passed down to his sons so they would not lose their identity. They almost faced extermination in Egypt at the cruel hands of Pharaoh, but they had hope in God to keep His promise. Eventually, He rescued them, and the nation of Israel was born the day they left Egypt to go to their own land as God had promised their forefathers.

4.3 Satan's Deception on Youths to Call Themselves Dogs

What did the Bible say about dogs? Biblical perspective on the nature and character of dogs is negative, and God will never call His children dogs. He will not be pleased with His children calling themselves dogs or manifesting the characteristics of a dog. This is not to say that dogs are not good animals or that God hates dogs. On the contrary, God said that everything He created is very good, and this includes dogs. What we are talking about here is spiritual and relates to the character of dogs. God detests any human being who manifests the nature and character of a dog. Here are some Bible verses that express God's position on the nature and characteristics of dogs.

Proverbs 26:11,

As a dog returneth to his vomit, so a fool returneth to his folly.

Matthew 7:6,

Give not that which is holy unto the dogs, neither cast ye your pearls before swine, lest they trample them under their feet, and turn again and rend you.

Matthew 15:26,

But he answered and said, it is not meet to take the children's bread, and to cast it to dogs.

Philippians 3:2,

Beware of dogs, beware of evil workers, beware of the concision.

Revelation 22:15,

For without are dogs, and sorcerers, and whoremongers, and murderers, and idolaters, and whosoever loveth and maketh a lie.

The Scriptures above reveal that God detests those who manifest the nature and characteristics of dogs and that they have no place in His kingdom. However, Satan has rewritten all that negativity in our time through music. We can see this, especially in the hip-hop music world, where young people happily proclaim and celebrate that they are dogs. Satan inspired rap music artists to use doggy stage names like Doggy Fresh, Snoop Dogg, Dog Pound, Lil Bow Wow, Pitbull, etc. He went further to inspire them and other music artists who do not have such names to glorify the nature and pleasure of the doggy lifestyle. Dogs and their nature and character are now glamorized and glorified. They and their followers openly proclaim that they are dogs, they put on dog chains and doggy pendants of all kinds. They glamorize the nature and characters of dogs and take pleasure in behaving like dogs. The same nature and character that God hates and says that those of such nature have no place in His Kingdom.

Revelation 22:15:

For without are dogs, and sorcerers, and whoremongers, and murderers, and idolaters, and whosoever loveth and maketh a lie.

Through music, Satan sent out demonic spirits to infest the human mind and body to manifest the characteristics of dogs in man. And what does this do in the lives of these singers and their listeners/fans? The more they confess that they are dogs, the more they invoke the demonic doggy spirit in them, taking them deeper and deeper into sin. Thereby alienating them further away from God and aligning them with hell and Satan. We must understand that name-calling is very important. When people profess themselves to be dogs, these demonic spirits take over them and begin to produce and manifest those doggy characters they glorify. This is one of the reasons you see so much sexual promiscuity and violence among these dog-glamorizing hip-hop artists and their fans. They find it normal and entertaining to engage in reckless sexual lifestyles with multiple partners. They unashamedly glamorize and glorify their doggy lifestyles. This is one of the reasons why there is so much promiscuity and violence in the hip-hop community, after all, dogs sleep around and fight each other "Dog eat Dog". They are just doing the doggy things because doggy demonic spirits have taken over them and are manifesting themselves through them.

4.4: How Did Humanity Arrive at Calling Their Children Goats (Kids)?

A kid is the young of a goat. God commanded in the Old Testament that the kid (young goat) be used for sin offering sacrifices. The children of Israel sacrificed kids (young goats) before the LORD as an offering for their sins, as documented in the Old Testament.

Leviticus 23:19

Then ye shall sacrifice one kid of the goats for a sin offering, and two lambs of the first year for a sacrifice of peace offerings.

Numbers 7:21-22

²¹One young bullock, one ram, one lamb of the first year, for a burnt offering: ²²One kid of the goats for a sin offering:

Satan is a counterfeiter of God's ways. The devil counterfeited this sacrifice, replacing the kid with a child, and requested child sacrifice from his worshippers. The Satanic world is known for the evil of sacrificing children to Satan. This evil of child sacrifice has been practiced for thousands of years by evil men and women in their idolatrous worship of Satan. This horrific practice spanned across all the continents of the world, from Europe among the Druids to South and Central America, to Asia, and Africa.

This horrific practice of satanic kingdoms is documented in the Bible and has been revealed by many ex-Satanists/occultic men and women in contemporary times. I recommend you watch Joseph Okechukwu's videos *"Shadows of Darkness Part 1, 2 & 3"* on Rumble to get a glimpse of what these evil satanic men and women do with children in secret.

Jeremiah 19:4-5

⁴Because they have forsaken me, and have estranged this place, and have burned incense in it unto other gods, whom neither they nor their fathers have known, nor the kings of Judah, and have filled this place with the blood of innocents; ⁵They have built also the high places of Baal, to burn their sons with fire for burnt offerings unto Baal, which I commanded not, nor spake it, neither came it into my mind:

Jeremiah 32:35

35And they built the high places of Baal, which are in the valley of the son of Hinnom, to cause their sons and their daughters to pass through the fire unto Molech; which I commanded them not, neither came it into my mind, that they should do this abomination, to cause Judah to sin.

The above Bible verses in Jeremiah and many others revealed the evil practice of child sacrifices by Satanists. God is saying that they have built altars to Baal and offered their sons as burnt offerings to Baal. The phrase *"to cause their sons and their daughters to pass through the fire unto Molech;"* in Jeremiah 32:35, does not mean that the children went through the fire and are alive on the other end. Molech is a god, the god of the Ammonites, and is a spirit. To pass through the fire unto Molech means to go through the fire into the spirit world to be with Molech. This means that the children were horrifically offered to Molech by burning them alive in the fire. The children entered the fire alive, died, and entered the spirit world to be with Molech. This understanding aligns with what God said earlier in Jeremiah 19:5, *"They have built also the high places of Baal, to burn their sons with fire for burnt offerings unto Baal,..."* 2Chronicles 28:1-3 clearly shows what it means to pass through the fire in the valley of the son of Hinnom, as stated in Jeremiah 32:35. It revealed that King Ahaz practiced this horrific satanic child sacrifice of burning children alive in the valley of the son of Hinnom.

2Chronicles 28:1-3

1Ahaz was twenty years old when he began to reign, and he reigned sixteen years in Jerusalem: but he did not that which was right in the sight of the LORD, like David his father: 2For he walked in the ways of the kings of Israel, and made also molten images for Baalim. 3Moreover he burnt incense in the valley of the son of Hinnom, and burnt his children in the fire, after the abominations of the heathen whom the LORD had cast out before the children of Israel.

Satanic men and women have been using children as sacrificial kids (young goats) for thousands of years. Could it be that calling children kids came from these satanic men and women in contemporary times as symbolism for their sacrificial kid (young goat)? Did calling children kids emanate from these evil people because children were their kids (young goats) for sacrifice? Did these satanic men and women code their discussions on their child sacrifices by saying they used a kid instead of a child? Most likely yes, just like satanic men and women like King Ahaz in Bible days called theirs "pass children through the fire" instead of "burning children alive in the fire". Satan is the father goat as revealed in the Scripture and also as symbolized by the image of Satan (Baphomet).

BAPHOMET
(Occultic anthropomorphic image of Satan with the head
and legs of a goat)

Matthew 25:32-34,41

[32]And before him shall be gathered all nations: and he shall separate them one from another, as a shepherd divideth his sheep from the goats: [33]And he shall set the sheep on his right hand, but the goats on the left. [34]Then shall the King say unto them on his right hand, Come, ye blessed of my Father, inherit the kingdom prepared for you from the

foundation of the world: [41]Then shall he say also unto them on the left hand, Depart from me, ye cursed, into everlasting fire, prepared for the devil and his angels:

Jesus said that all goats will be cast into hellfire with their father Satan on the last day. He said that He will gather all nations and separate them into two categories: sheep and goats. The sheep He will put on His right hand and the goats on His left. The sheep on His right hand are blessed and are His, and He will bring them into His Kingdom. But the goats on His left are cursed and are Satan's, and He will cast them into everlasting fire (hellfire) to be with the devil for eternity. This Bible passage shows that goats are the children of the devil and will eventually end up in hellfire for eternity with their father Satan. If goats are the children of Satan, then calling children goats (kids) could not have been inspired by God. The name goat (kid) is the opposite of what God called His children. Surely, calling children goats is inspired by Satan, the father of all goats. And he has used his kiddifying agents like music, social media, TV, cartoons, and celebrities to promote and glamorize calling children kids (goats). Could calling our children goats (kids) be casting spells on them, dedicating them to Satan, and invoking the death-giving goat spirit into them, the spirit of stubbornness and rebellion? Or is it just a harmless nomenclature to call our children (goats) kids? Have your children been Kiddified? That is to say, turned into spiritual goats and dedicated to Satan for eternal damnation in hellfire.

4.5: Unmasking How Calling Children "Kids" Stimulates Negative Behaviors

When you call your children "kids." It is not just a nice way of calling them goats. Unknown to you over time, your perception will be conditioned spiritually to view them as goats. In other words, you will not see anything wrong with them manifesting the stubborn and rebellious characters of goats. You will not see it necessary to train them to desist from such characters. You will assume it to be their nature and okay for them to behave that way. Your mindset would be to leave them alone because they are just kids (goats). They will become goats to you spiritually, and consequently, you will treat them as such (Not train them appropriately). On the other hand, you will continually dedicate them to Satan by invoking the death-giving goat spirit into them as you call them kids (goats). They will eventually become Kiddified and grow up to become "big kids (big goats)" that is, adult goats.

Matthew 25:33-34, 41

[33]And he shall set the SHEEP ON HIS RIGHT HAND, but the GOATS ON THE LEFT. [34]Then shall the King say unto them on his right hand, Come, ye blessed of my Father, inherit the kingdom prepared for you from the foundation of the world: [41]Then shall he say also unto them on the LEFT HAND, Depart from me, ye cursed, into everlasting fire, prepared for the devil and his angels:

Goats are stubborn and rebellious; they have the character of witchcraft because rebellion is like the sin of witchcraft. Goats are known for their stubbornness, and many are familiar with the term "Stubborn goat," usually used to describe a stubborn person. The Bible in 1Samuel 15:23 says, ***"For rebellion is as the sin of witchcraft, and stubbornness is as iniquity and idolatry. Because thou hast rejected the word of the LORD, he hath also rejected thee from being king."*** Stubbornness equates to the sin of idolatry, and the idol worshipped is the father goat- Satan. The spiritual reality is that goats – the Kiddified (Those with goatlike character) have no place in the kingdom of God.

I believe you now understand that it is the devil who came up with the idea that parents should call their children goats (kids). You can clearly see that this is the devil's character of countering whatever God says or does with the very opposite, like he is doing with marriage, creation, gender, etc. Jesus called His children sheep and called the devil's children goats. Then the devil used satanic men and women, entertainment industries, the media, and social media, and enticed parents to start calling their children goats (kids). Why did the world not call them lamb if it is just a harmless name? It is because the devil is in the details; he is the spirit behind calling children kids. The devil is the spirit that is behind opposing whatever God says or does. The devil is the one behind calling evil good and good evil; putting darkness for light and light for darkness; calling sweet, bitter, and bitter, sweet. He deceives humanity to do so because he knows that God's damnation awaits those who do such.

Isaiah 5:20

Woe unto them that call evil good, and good evil; that put darkness for light, and light for darkness; that put bitter for sweet, and sweet for bitter!

Have you ever wondered why the devil's image of Baphomet is that of a goat? Yes, the devil is the father goat and has manipulated parents to cast spells and dedicate their children to him by calling them baby goats (kids). Calling your children kids (goats) cast spells on them, and dedicate them to the devil. It invokes the death-giving goat spirit into them – the spirit of stubbornness and rebellion, which is the spirit of the devil. The devil knows that goats will burn with him in hell for all of eternity. That is why he deceived parents to raise their children like goats so that on the last day, they would hear what Jesus said in Matthew 25:33,41, *³³And he shall set the sheep on his right hand, but the GOATS ON THE LEFT. ⁴¹Then shall he say also unto them on the left hand, Depart from me, ye cursed, into everlasting fire, prepared for the devil and his angels:*

Jesus said we should bring our children to Him. Unfortunately, many parents have made their children goats spiritually and are laboring hard to bring goats to Jesus. Goats cannot come to Jesus; they are stubborn and rebellious like their father, the devil. If you can be honest with yourself, you would have observed these two characters in your children that you have unknowingly labeled as goats. Jesus says we should bring our children to Him and not goats. He said that the Kingdom of God is for children and not goats. Therefore, do not alienate your children from the kingdom of God by dedicating them continually to Satan and invoking the hell-bound death-giving goat spirit into them by calling them kids (goats).

Luke 18:16

But Jesus called them unto him, and said, Suffer little children to come unto me, and forbid them not: for of such is the kingdom of God.

However, it is not really the name kid by itself that condemns children to the ungodly goat's behaviors of stubbornness and rebellion. Rather, it is the subtle reprogramming or retraining of the minds of parents in a way that has caused a paradigm shift in how they think and relate to their children. Your children are not necessarily behaving like goats simply because you are calling them goats (kids). You could still call them children and still treat them as goats, and they will behave like goats. Children are born in a fallen state because man fell from glory in the Garden of Eden. Therefore, children are born with innate mischief or foolishness.

Proverbs 22:15

Foolishness is bound in the heart of a child; but the rod of correction shall drive it far from him.

The devil's goal was to produce a paradigm shift in belief on how people view and relate to their children by selling this idea of calling children kids (goats) to parents. This kid (goat) calling became prominent in the 1840s and was glamorized in the early sixties and seventies. Christians, especially in America, withstood it for a while but later gave in. Unfortunately, the devil succeeded in his goal to create a paradigm shift in how parents view and relate to their children. If you have ever been around real kids, that is the young of goats, you will perfectly understand what took place. Baby goats just jump around playfully until they become adult goats. They do not need any training; they just jump around playfully until they grow to become stubborn adult goats.

Satan aimed to subtly work on parents and children psychologically to produce his desired results. He created a paradigm shift in belief and understanding of how parents should deal with their children. So instead of training them appropriately, they will excuse their ungodly stubborn characters and say, "They are just kids (goats). Instead of disciplining them promptly when they misbehave, they excuse their bad behaviors and say, "They are just kids (goats)." Why? Because parents have been conditioned in their minds to think of them as kids (goats), and the children are being destroyed. Calling children kids (goats) affects parents internally by changing their understanding and perspective on training their children. Then it affects the children externally by the way parents train their children because of their goat (kid)-skewed perspective of their children. Then it affects the children internally as they observe their parents ignore and condone some of their bad behaviors. Making them believe that they are just kids (goats) and that it is okay for them to act mischievous and stubborn. Therefore, they grow up believing their bad characters are normal and acceptable. Their parents have caused them to stray because Satan conditioned them to call their children goats (kids) and treat them as such.

I traveled to North Dakota in 2021 for a revival program we organized, and after the church service on Sunday, we came out for coffee and snacks. While we stood in the queue for coffee and snacks, some of our children just noisily ran to the front and were about to start grabbing snacks. I rebuked them and asked them to be orderly and do the right thing by joining the queue. Then one sister said: "Let them be; they are just kids." But I objected, telling her and the children that they were not kids but children and had to follow the same principles of life, behave orderly, and join the queue to be served. Then the sister sarcastically said to me Okay, Mr. Daddy. The children gladly joined the queue and got their snacks and drinks. From this story, you can clearly see the kid-skewed view of that sister and how it was affecting the children. She sees it okay for the children to behave rowdy and disorderly because they are just kids (goats). She finds it needless to train them and sees their behaviors as acceptable because they are just kids (goats). The children felt it was acceptable for them to be rowdy and disorderly because they knew that people viewed them as just kids (goats) and that it was perfectly okay for them to behave that way.

Kids or young goats are not meant to be trained. So, they playfully jump around and kid around until they become big kids (goats). That is why you hear people say "I am just kidding around", yes, that is what real kids (young goats) do, they kid around. The Bible says to train up a child, not a kid. Goats are born and allowed to jump around playfully until they become adult goats. Calling children kids is just programming them to become spiritual goats who will not receive training or discipline. They grow bodily but remain the same in their character. You might have heard parents or adults say of a child, "He is just a big kid." Unknowingly to them, they are simply saying, he is just a big goat (he wasn't trained).

What God achieved in Jacob and his family by changing Jacob's name to Israel is what Satan achieved in most parents and children today by getting parents to call their children "kids". When parents call their children goats (kids), they create a wrong identity of their children in their minds and that of their children.

"Oh, they are just kids (goats), "some parents say, allowing their children to go unpunished, unsupervised, untrained, and wayward. The power of confession; you often get what you profess with your mouth Num 14:28, **"Say unto them, as truly as I live, saith the LORD, as ye have spoken in mine ears, so will I do to you:"** Therefore, confess positively, speak right things, and rightly call your offsprings, children.

You could still call your offspring children. But in your mind, you still see them as goats and consequently treat them as such. Therefore, the most important thing is not changing what you call them, but deprogramming your mind from the "Just a kid (goat)" mentality. Then reprogram your mind to see them as the children that the LORD called them, and position your heart to train them. Proverbs 22:6 *"Train up a child in the way he should go: and when he is old, he will not depart from it."* Remember that life and death are in the power of the tongue. Proverbs 18:21, *"Death and life are in the power of the tongue: and they that love it shall eat the fruit thereof."* PLEASE CALL YOUR GOD-GIVEN OFFSPRING CHILDREN AND NOT GOATS.

CHAPTER 5

Don't Kiddify Your Children

Don't Kiddify Your Children is a follow-up principle to *call them children and not Kids*. As we have seen so far, Satan's agenda is to make you 'Kiddify' your children in your thoughts and understanding, thereby making you believe that all they need to develop into functional adults is all the kiddy stuff he promotes through his various agents. All these are in his effort to lay the foundation of your children's lives and condition their minds to conform to his evil world's thought process. The Bible admonishes that we should not be conformed to this world.

Romans 12:2

And be not conformed to this world: but be ye transformed by the renewing of your mind, that ye may prove what is that good, and acceptable, and perfect, will of God.

"Be not" in this verse speaks of proactive and active measures to resist conformity to this world. This also implies that there are expected negative occurrences, maneuvers, deception, and proactive and active plans to get one to conform to this world. Satan is the ruler of this world's evil system, and his goal is to get humanity to conform to his world system of thoughts. Since humans are governed by their thought processes, the end result is sinful habits and lifestyles.

For this reason, Satan has employed and deployed many mind-programming devices in the world to accomplish his task. These mind-programming devices include social media, music, TV, cartoons, video games, dolls, etc. Therefore, parents are deceived into leaving the most valuable period of training for their children in the hands of Satan through social media, music, TV, cartoons, video games, and other 'kiddifying' Satanic devices like dolls, etc. Then through all his kiddifying devices, Satan ends up raising young kids and big kids for Christian parents. That is to say, young goats and big goats, Kiddified children—untrained children who do not know the LORD nor care about the things of the LORD.

Hosea 5:5-7

5And the pride of Israel doth testify to his face: therefore shall Israel and Ephraim fall in their iniquity; Judah also shall fall with them. 6They shall go with their flocks and with their herds to seek the LORD; but they shall not find him; he hath withdrawn himself from them. 7They have dealt treacherously against the LORD: FOR THEY HAVE BEGOTTEN STRANGE CHILDREN: now shall a month devour them with their portions.

God was reproving the children of Israel for raising strange children for Him. One thing we should know about our God is that He is highly interested in children. That is why He said in Matthew 19:14, **"... Suffer little children, and forbid them not, to come unto me: for of such is the kingdom of heaven."**

The LORD is highly interested in godly offspring. When the Lord says He hates divorce, it is because He desires godly offspring. He desires godly children. So, when you abandon your children to TV, music, social media, video games, dolls, and other Satan's kiddifying devices. You have succeeded in handing over your children to Satan to train them. Subsequently, you have failed to observe God's commandment, which says you should train them to fear and honor Him.

Malachi 2:15-16

15And did not he make one? Yet had he the residue of the spirit. And wherefore one? THAT HE MIGHT SEEK A GODLY SEED. Therefore take heed to your spirit, and let none deal treacherously against the wife of his youth. 16For the LORD, the God of Israel, saith that he hateth putting away: for one covereth violence with his garment, saith the LORD of hosts: therefore take heed to your spirit, that ye deal not treacherously.

Genesis 18:19

For I know him, that he will command his children and his household after him, and they shall keep the way of the LORD, to do justice and judgment; that the LORD may bring upon Abraham that which he hath spoken of him.

God spoke confidently of Abraham that He knows he will raise his children in the way of the LORD. God said, "For I know him, that he will command his children…" This means that Abraham will stand his ground on godly training for his children, speaking boldly and authoritatively to ensure his children follow the way of the LORD. Training children requires time and resources; Abraham and Sarah must have sacrificed time and resources to accomplish this.

The children of Israel failed to train their children in the ways of the Lord. Their children could not come to the LORD because they were goats who were stubborn and rebellious and would not answer the call of the LORD. They raised children whom God could not recognize; strange children. How could this have happened? They abandoned their children in the hands of Satan in pursuit of wealth and the pleasures of the heathen nations.

Malachi 5:5-7

⁵And the pride of Israel doth testify to his face: therefore shall Israel and Ephraim fall in their iniquity; Judah also shall fall with them. ⁶They shall go with their flocks and with their herds to seek the LORD; but they shall not find him; he hath withdrawn himself from them. ⁷They have dealt treacherously against the LORD: for they have begotten strange children: now shall a month devour them with their portions.

Many parents have employed these Satan's kiddifying devices as their babysitters because they are too busy running after careers and dollars. When they are home, they are too tired and engaged with other things that need attention. Therefore, they rely on these kiddifying devices for babysitting. If you abandon your children to social media, music, TV, Cartoons, video games, dolls, and other Santan's kiddifying devices because you are busy running after things of minimal value compared to your children. You will end up with kiddified children who are estranged from the LORD. Kiddified children are untrained children who do not fear the LORD nor care about the things of God. Children who hate the ways of the LORD.

5.1 Negative Effects of Worldly Music on Children

Music! Music! Music!!! I am referring to worldly music. There is no greater satanic programming and kiddifying agent than worldly music. One of the greatest, if not the greatest of all the devices of Satan in programming people's minds to conform to his desired worldview is music. This does not pertain to children alone but to people of all ages. Music activates almost every part of the brain, from the limbic to the motor systems. Therefore, it increases blood flow to the region of the brain that generates emotions. It activates and keeps memories alive and drives the motor system to move the listener into action. This is why people are moved to dance, tap their hands, or nod their heads to the sound of music. The three major components of the effect of music on its listeners are Emotion, Memory Retention, and Action. Music activates the emotions of its listeners, helps them to remember the message, and moves them to action. Music could be a great asset that can be used to positively shape a person's character when the message of the music is good, rational, and positive.

This is why some of the Words of God in the Bible are given to us in Psalms and songs. God inspired Moses to compose a song about the victory God gave them at the Red Sea over the Egyptians so they never forget, Exodus chapter 15. Also, shortly before God asked Moses to go to Mount Abarim to die, He gave Moses a very important message for the children of Israel as a song so that they would not forget it; Deuteronomy 32. I remember struggling with the spelling of correction as a child, and my mother spelled it for me in a song format, and from that day forward, it never departed from me. This was why King Lemuel's mother gave him the most important lessons for his life and success in a song format. His mother gave him the lesson as a song to stir up his emotions and cause him to always remember the lessons. In order to move him to take the right actions in life. Music triggers meditation and causes the listener to constantly think about the message of the music. It is difficult to forget a message given as a song because as the receiver repeats the song, the message is engraved in their subconscious mind. Gradually, the message of the music will ultimately shape their worldview and character.

King Lemuel: Proverbs 31:1-5

¹The words of king Lemuel, the prophecy that his mother taught him. ²What, my son? and what, the son of my womb? and what, the son of my vows? ³Give not thy strength unto women, nor thy ways to that which destroyeth kings. ⁴It is not for kings, O Lemuel, it is not for kings to drink wine; nor for princes strong drink: ⁵Lest they drink, and forget the law, and pervert the judgment of any of the afflicted.

In the eighteenth century, Andrew Fletcher of Scotland said, *"Let me make the songs of a nation, and I care not who makes its laws."* There is great insight into the effect of music on its listeners in this saying. This does not imply that laws are unimportant; of course, one will either be justified or condemned by the law, whether the laws of God or those of nations. This saying reveals the fact that the person who controls the music of a nation controls the people's character and determines the culture of the land. The three major components of the effect of music on its listeners are Emotion, Memory Retention, and Action. Music activates the emotions of its listeners, helps them to remember and retain the message, and moves them to action. The message of the music is easily engraved in the listener's subconscious mind through the arousal of emotion (passion) and repetition. This ultimately shapes the person's worldview and character. Unfortunately, this great tool of character molding called music is in the very hands of Satan. Satan is highly skilled in music, and he is the inspiration behind worldly music. His goal is to shape and control the character and culture of the nations to the eternal damnation of the people's souls in hell.

Isaiah 14:10-12

¹⁰They all shall speak and say to you: 'Have you also become as weak as we? Have you become like us? ¹¹Your pomp is brought down to Sheol, AND THE SOUND OF YOUR STRINGED INSTRUMENTS; The maggot is spread under you, And worms cover you.' ¹²"How you are fallen from heaven, O Lucifer, son of the morning! How you are cut down to the ground, You who weakened the nations! (NKJV)

The Bible verses above speak of the fall and the impending eternal judgment in hell of Lucifer, a.k.a Satan and the Devil. His musical skills are referenced in verse 11, *"and the sound of your stringed instruments."* Note, "instruments" with the "s" Satan is the master musician, diversely skilled in all types of musical instruments. He is the master instrumentalist, creating and inspiring the lyrics and melodies of worldly music. His goal is to mold the character and culture of the nations to the damnation of the people's souls in hellfire.

Before becoming a Christian, the strongest influence that shaped my ungodly philosophies and characters was music; hip hop/rap music in particular, especially the songs of Snoop Dogg.

One of those Snoop Dogg's songs that really altered my character for the worse was Gin and Juice. Here is a sample of the lyrics: *"Keep rolling down the streets smoking indo (marijuana) sipping on gin and juice; laid back, with my mind on my money and my money on my mind."* Is this not a message inspired by Satan from hell? This lyrics sample of Snoop Dogg's "Gin and Juice" is saintly compared to some other lyrics, especially those of current hip hop/rap music. Snoop Dogg's Gin and Juice song changed my view on marijuana, alcohol, and money. As I continuously played and sang the song, the message was engraved in my subconscious mind, and it ultimately shaped my character. I started to consume marijuana and gin and juice, and made money, my god. All glory to God Almighty; my LORD and Savior Jesus Christ, who delivered me from the grip of Satan.

Although the Bible condemned and characterized the nature of dogs as ungodly and evil. Notwithstanding, Satan, through the power and influence of worldly music, was able to inspire and influence children to call themselves dogs and behave like dogs. God will never call His children dogs and will not be pleased with humans He created in His image calling themselves dogs or manifesting the characteristics of a dog. God does not hate dogs, and dogs are good animals because God said that everything He created is very good and this includes dogs; Genesis 1:31. However, God detests any human being that manifests the nature and character of a dog because it is evil for humans to behave like dogs.

Proverbs 26:11

As a dog returneth to his vomit, so a fool returneth to his folly.

Matthew 7:6

Give not that which is holy unto the dogs, neither cast ye your pearls before swine, lest they trample them under their feet, and turn again and rend you.

Philippians 3:2

Beware of dogs, beware of evil workers, beware of the concision.

Revelation 22:15

For without are dogs, and sorcerers, and whoremongers, and murderers, and idolaters, and whosoever loveth and maketh a lie.

God detests those who manifest the nature and characteristics of dogs, and they have no place in His kingdom. However, Satan has rewritten the negativity about the characteristics of a dog in our time through worldly music. This we can see in the hip-hop/rap music world, where young people happily proclaim and celebrate that they are dogs. The artists and their followers openly proclaim that they are dogs, they put on dogs' chains and doggy pendants of all kinds. Satan inspired rap artists to use doggy stage names like Doggy Fresh, Snoop Dogg, Dog Pound, Lil Bow Wow, Pitbull, etc. They have glamorized and glorified the characteristics of a dog as a human lifestyle; a thing which God hates. When children continuously listen to and sing these songs, the message will be engraved in their subconscious mind and will ultimately shape their character. What are the characteristics of dogs? Violence, Dominance, Promiscuity, and living just for pleasure.

Through worldly music, demonic spirits infest the human mind and body to manifest the characteristics of dogs. The more these singers and their listeners/fans confess that they are dogs, the more they invoke the demonic doggy spirit in them, taking them deeper and deeper into sin. Thereby alienating them further away from God and aligning them with hell and Satan. This is why there is so much sexual promiscuity and violence among these dog-glamorizing hip-hop/rap artists and their fans. It is absolutely normal and entertaining for them to engage in reckless sexual lifestyles with multiple partners. They unashamedly glamorize and glorify their doggy lifestyles through music. Music activates and keeps memories alive and drives the motor system to move the listener into action. This is why you find little girls twerking (sexually provocative dance) and ten-year-old girls getting pregnant; Kiddified children. This is why there is so much sexual promiscuity and violence in the hip-hop community, after all, dogs sleep around and fight each other "Dog eat Dog". They behave like dogs because the doggy demonic spirits have taken over them through the power and influence of worldly music. Andrew Fletcher: *"Let me make the songs of a nation, and I care not who makes its laws."* The person who controls the music of a nation controls the people's character and determines the culture of the land. The one obviously controlling the music of the nations is Satan. Christian parents who desire to raise godly children must shield their children from being Kiddified through worldly music.

5.2 Negative Effects of TV and Cartoons on Children

Several TV shows and cartoons encourage ungodly behaviors in children. They give ungodly messages to children. They contain sexual innuendos and sexual scenes, encourage aggression, and promote stubbornness and rebellion in children. These TV shows and cartoons affect children's behavior and make them think it is normal to be aggressive, spoiled, stubborn, rebellious, violent, and sexually immoral.

According to AACAP (American Academy of Child and Adolescent Psychiatry), *"Children who view shows in which violence is very realistic, frequently repeated, or unpunished are more likely to imitate what they see. The child's brain and eyes are usually affected by the speed of the images affects."* Have you ever wondered why children in the 21st Century are always bored? Their commonly used vocabulary is "I am bored, it's boring." This is because, for the most part, they are always engaged with the unreal world of cartoons and video games. In this unreal world, life is very fast, and characters move very quickly. They become so used to the high-speed image affects of these cartoons and video game characters that real life becomes too slow for them and boring. Therefore, they are always bored with almost everything in real life until they are re-engaged with their unreal world.

This research by AACAP reveals that shows with high-speed image affects, in which violence is very realistic, frequently repeated, or unpunished, destroy children's character, brain, and eyes. According to AACAP, children who view such shows are more likely to imitate what they see. It is the same God-given natural principle in training a child that is at play. Proverbs 22:6,

"Train up a child in the way he should go: and when he is old, he will not depart from it."

Early Years Psychology says, "Give me the child until he is seven and I will make him what you want him to be." This psychology says ages 0-7 are the formative years of a child; that is, character molding-wise. Everything else we do after age zero to seven to mold the character of a child cannot be foundational and may not last. The philosophy is, "The earlier the better." It is the same God-given natural principle of training a child that is at work here. Proverbs 22:6, **"Train up a child in the way he should go: and when he is old, he will not depart from it."** Satan knows that the children will not depart from his desired lifestyle if he succeeds in shaping them in knowledge and character at the foundational stage –Ground-Zero, (age 0-7). The world and Satan understand this God-given natural principle and take due advantage of it. This is why Satan deceived parents into believing that all their children needed to grow and mature were these kiddifying devices. So, parents could abandon their children to him through those devices.

While AACAP is more focused on violence and the physical defects caused by TV shows and cartoons. Heavenly-minded Christian parents should also be concerned about the spiritual effects of these TV shows and cartoons on their children. What other ungodly behaviors have you observed in TV shows and cartoons that are very realistic, frequently repeated, and unpunished? Make your list.... tantrum, lying, stealing, stubbornness, rebellion, vulgar language, gay, lesbianism, genderfluidity, transgenderism, sexual acts and sexual innuendos, etc.

Your Children will imitate these ungodly characters and much more if you abandon them to TV shows and cartoons. These characters will form the foundation of their lives, and they will most likely not depart from them. TV shows and cartoons are Satan's mind-programming devices in the world to accomplish his task of raising children who are alienated from God. If you leave the most valuable period of training your children in the hands of Satan through TV shows and cartoons. Satan will succeed in raising young goats and big goats for you, Kiddified children—untrained children who do not know the LORD nor care about the things of the LORD.

5.3 Negative Effects of Video Games on Children

Video games have all the negative effects of cartoons plus a stronger addictive tendency, which affects the intellectual development of children. Video games are cartoons 2.0; they are cartoons on steroids. This is so because the children now assume the character role in the cartoon; they are playing the character roles themselves. This makes video gaming more addictive and damaging to children. The high-speed image affects, glorified violent acts, and sexual acts in most of these video games are on steroids. Then you could only imagine how damaging they are to children, knowing that they now impersonate those characters. When a child is playing any video game, they impersonate the character in the game; the child becomes that character. It becomes very personal for the child and ultimately affects his thinking and character. This is why video gaming is very addictive, and a child would do anything, give up, and abandon whatever just to spend endless time playing video games.

I fully understand the addictive and damaging effects of video games on children, even when it is seemingly harmless games like sports and so on. I know this because I witnessed it for myself while in secondary school and while doing business in Nigeria. During my secondary school days in Ikeja, Nigeria. Students will leave school during school hours to Allen Avenue in Ikeja, to play video games. Most of these students will steal their parents' money in thousands and will waste it all playing video games. Some will steal their parents' properties like jewelry, electronics, and whatever is of value, sell them, and waste the money on gaming and other things. Some of the games they played were violent, while some were just regular nonviolent games. Nonetheless, the effect on them was all the same. It was addictive, and the children would do anything, give up, and abandon whatever just to spend endless time playing video games. They stole their parents' money and properties, abandoned classes, and risked the consequences of their theft, and of abandoning school, if or when they got caught. Most of these students did not do as well in school as they ought to have done. They wasted class time, study time, and homework time playing video games.

I witnessed this game center where these students usually go to play games make millions from these children. I knew this because I had been to the game joint on one or two occasions, and also from students talking about the games they played and how much money they spent playing games. I also know this because I later got to know the person who managed that game center after I started my own business. We became friends and talked about how much money they used to make from the game center when he was the manager. Being naturally business-minded, I knew that there was a lot of money to be made in gaming right from my secondary school days. I knew because the victims are addicted and are willing to part with any amount just to get their high and the next high.

Knowing that there is a lot of money to be made in the gaming business, I delved into it after secondary school. I was not disappointed; I made a lot of money. It was through the gaming business that I made enough money to start traveling abroad to import game consoles like Sony PlayStation and Super Nintendo and their accessories. I witnessed children sit in my gaming center from morning to evening/night playing games. When their money finishes, they will quickly go home and return with more money. They would steal their parents' money and spend it at my game center. They wasted most of their day at my game center and were not very useful to their parents, nor did they have time to do things that would add value to their lives, like studying. I did not care then because I did not know any better; all I wanted was to make money. Knowing what I know now, I would never have gone into such an ungodly business. These children were behaving like drug addicts. They would spend their food money on gaming at my game center. They stole their parents' money and properties, abandoned classes, and risked the consequences just to get their high and the next high in gaming.

5.4 Negative Effects of Dolls on Children

The eyes are a gateway to a person's life. Whatever goes in through the eyes ultimately shapes a person's character and lifestyle. This is a natural principle. Whatever goes in through the eyes-gateway has the potential to shape one's life through the thought process. The things people see are processed through thoughts to form opinions that may settle in the heart and shape one's character and perspective on life. Jacob understood this principle of life and used this powerful tool to convert almost all of Laban's flocks to become his.

Jacob has been serving Laban, his father-in-law, for many years, and Laban has been changing their agreement just to keep Jacob serving him perpetually. After Jacob's wife gave birth to Joseph, he asked Laban to send him away to start his own life with his family. However, Laban wanted to convince Jacob to continue to stay and serve him because he knew that God was blessing him because of Jacob. He asked Jacob to name his wages in order to stay and continue serving him. Jacob suggested that he let him keep all the flocks that were brown, speckled, and spotted among the sheep, goats, and cattle as his wages. Laban quickly grabbed this deal because these colors are not usually common among the flocks. Laban knew that all things being equal, it was a wonderful deal for him as Jacob would only end up getting very little flocks as his wages. He never knew that Jacob had a game plan that had been proven to be very successful.

Genesis 30:37-43

³⁰And Jacob took him rods of green poplar, and of the hazel and chesnut tree; and pilled white strakes in them, and made the white appear which was in the rods. ³⁸And he set the rods which he had pilled before the flocks in the gutters in the watering troughs when the flocks came to drink, that they should conceive when they came to drink ³⁹And the flocks conceived before the rods, and brought forth cattle ringstraked, speckled, and spotted. ⁴⁰And Jacob did separate the lambs, and set the faces of the flocks toward the ringstraked, and all the brown in the flock of Laban; and he put his own flocks by themselves, and put them not unto Laban's cattle. ⁴¹And it came to pass, whensoever the stronger cattle did conceive, that Jacob laid the rods before the eyes of the cattle in the gutters, that they might conceive among the rods. ⁴²But when the cattle were feeble, he put them not in: so the feebler were Laban's, and the stronger Jacob's. ⁴³And the man increased exceedingly, and had much cattle, and maidservants, and menservants, and camels, and asses.

Jacob took rods of green poplar, hazel, and chestnut trees and peeled white strips in them to create ringstraked, speckled, and spotted rods. He would then place these rods before the flocks in the watering troughs where the flocks came to drink water. As the flocks constantly see these rods as they drink water and conceive, it passes a coded message to design the baby that is being formed in the womb. Because the eyes are a gateway, these coded messages that their eyes constantly send internally are being decoded and processed as beauty and sent to design the forming baby in the womb. Therefore, when the flocks gave birth, their offspring are ringstraked, speckled, and spotted. Jacob used this natural principle to convert almost all of Laban's flocks to his own.

Many people are familiar with the saying "You are what you eat," and few are familiar with "You are what you hear," but most people are not familiar with "You are what you see." These sayings are true because the mouth, ears, and eyes are gateways to a person's life. Whatever goes into a person through the mouth, ears, and eyes has the potential to shape the outcome of that person's life. Jacob exploited the eyes-gateway and succeeded in converting most of Laban's flocks to become his own. Satan has also exploited, and still is exploiting the eyes-gateway, and has succeeded, and is still succeeding in converting most of God's creation to become his.

Have you ever wondered how it became possible for a rational mind to fix fake eyelashes and think it made her beautiful? If you were told twenty years ago that normal human beings would buy fake eyelashes with their money and glue them to their eyes for beauty, would you have believed? How did women arrive at this debased mindset of believing that gluing fake eyelashes to their eyes is a rational act of beautification? Have you ever wondered how the human mind got so debased to see a half-naked lady to be hot and beautiful instead of shameful? Have you ever wondered why women gravitate towards adding everything artificial to a natural body, from makeup to fake hair, fake nails, etc., and think it is beautiful? Have you ever wondered how a supposedly rational mind arrived at dying his/her hair pink, purple, yellow, green, red, etc., and sees it as beautiful? You really do not have to think for long or look very far to find the answers. It all started with the dolls.

Just like Jacob, Satan engineered the creation of dolls with these naturally unrealistic beauty features like very large eyelashes. Painted their nails and dressed them half-naked. Then with the help of parents, he positioned them before the children continually. Satan had positioned these images before the children from their infancy as the image of beauty, just like Jacob positioned the ringstraked, speckled, and spotted rods before Laban's flocks, and they caused Laban's flocks to birth ringstraked, speckled, and spotted offspring. In the same way, Satan has positioned these dolls before God's creation and caused God's children to raise strange children for the LORD. Malachi 5:7, *"They have dealt treacherously against the LORD: for they have begotten strange children: now shall a month devour them with their portions."* As the children constantly behold, admire, and play with these dolls, coded messages are transmitted into their senses through the eyes' gateway. Therefore, these messages are then decoded by the child's brain to mean, "This is the standard of beauty, this is what is called beautiful, you must look like this to be called beautiful." The child is being trained non-verbally in their foundational stage through these doll images. The child internalizes all that he or she is receiving, and it forms the foundation of his or her life, which the child will not depart from except for a divine intervention. Proverbs 22:6, ***"Train up a child in the way he should go: and when he is old, he will not depart from it."***

When the female child grows up, it is already laid in her on the foundational level that putting on everything artificial and dressing half-naked is the standard of beauty, and that she must look like that to be called beautiful. While the males are wired at their foundational stage to only appreciate, admire, lust after, and compliment females who are dressed half-naked and are artificially made-up. And which woman does not want to be called beautiful? She will absolutely see nothing wrong with dressing as such, and the sense of it being shameful and embarrassing will not be there at all. Therefore, when she goes to the store, she is looking for the clothing that will make her beautiful by the standard she was trained through these satanic dolls. When Satan later on down the road introduces fake eyelashes, she would have no problem jumping at them because they fit her perfect description of beauty, as she observed in these dolls growing up. Satan will also shrewdly roll out these ungodly adornments that he has introduced through inanimate objects like dolls, cartoons, and pictures, through celebrities of all kinds. What the children have been seeing and admiring in these dolls and ungodly celebrities has gone through their thought process to form opinions and shape their perspective on beauty in life. It has set their standard for beauty and acceptable clothing. Parents who truly want to raise godly children must guard their children from beholding images that will destroy their moral foundations, and this includes these ungodly dolls and TV shows with these ungodly celebrities.

5.5 The Perils of Ungodly Adornments

Some people may ask, what is wrong with half-naked dressings and adding everything artificial to a natural body, from makeup to fake hair, fake nails, tattoos, etc., and dying one's hair pink, purple, yellow, green, red, etc.? It is paramount for Christian parents to understand the danger associated with these ungodly adornments that are being peddled to children through these ungodly dolls and celebrities of all kinds. However, there are Christians for this world, to whom heaven is not their ultimate goal. They don't regularly think of heaven and how to make it there with their family. They are Christians in name only and not in practice. They want both God and the world; they don't want to be separated from the world. They love the world and the things of the world. They want to live their best life now, which is only possible if hell is their final destination.

1 John 2:15-18

[15]Love not the world, neither the things that are in the world. If any man love the world, the love of the Father is not in him. [16]For all that is in the world, the lust of the flesh, and the lust of the eyes, and the pride of life, is not of the Father, but is of the world. [17]And the world passeth away, and the lust thereof: but he that doeth the will of God abideth for ever.

James 4:4

Ye adulterers and adulteresses, know ye not that the friendship of the world is enmity with God? whosoever therefore will be a friend of the world is the enemy of God.

If you are such a Christian, then what is being explained here does not concern you; as a matter of fact, this entire book is not relevant to you. Nevertheless, you may choose to repent and ask God for forgiveness. Change the trajectory of your life and refocus on making heaven with your family. Your soul and those of your children are the most valuable assets you possess in this life. They are your only assets with the potential of eternal value. If you bring them under the subjection of the Word of God, they will have eternal value, and you and your children will rejoice in heaven forever. You cannot afford to lose your soul or those of your family in hellfire for all eternity. However, if heaven is the ultimate goal for you and your family, then pay good attention to every issue discussed in this book.

1Corinthians 9:27

But I keep under my body, and bring it into subjection: lest that by any means, when I have preached to others, I myself should be a castaway.

Matthew 16:26

For what is a man profited, if he shall gain the whole world, and lose his own soul? or what shall a man give in exchange for his soul?

Adornments include all things done and materials put on the human body to achieve decency, beauty, and attractiveness, like hair plating, clothes, etc. Adornments are not bad altogether, otherwise, we would all be walking about naked. God wants His children to adorn themselves with modest clothing with the consciousness of not dressing in a manner that comes across as shameful. He wants Christians to make their choices in adornment with sobriety, avoiding ungodliness such as broided hair (weaving in ornament/artificial hair), jewelry, and ostentatious clothing.

1Timothy 2:9-10

⁹In like manner also, that women adorn themselves in modest apparel, with shamefacedness and sobriety; not with broided hair, or gold, or pearls, or costly array; ¹⁰But (which becometh women professing godliness) with good works.

What makes any bodily adornment ungodly is if it goes against the principles of God's Word. Satan, for centuries, has used dolls, music artists, TV hosts, sports stars, and influential figures to influence the world and Christians into the use of ungodly adornments. Ungodly adornments include but are not limited to, half-naked clothing, Jewelry, hair attachments, make-up, fake eyelashes, fake nails, hair dyeing, artificial body part implants, tattoos, bleaching cream, etc. These types of adornment are ungodly because they go against the Word of God and mock God's creative mastermind.

If we want to know the truth about any subject matter on life's existence, and acceptable human relationships and moral standards with each other and God, then we must go to the beginning. The book of Genesis is the Bible's account of the beginning of all creation. It holds lots of keys to unlocking and understanding biblical truth and mysteries. The LORD Jesus referenced the beginning, that is, Genesis, for divine authority and truth when the Pharisees tempted him on the issue of divorce. He referenced the beginning for divine authority and truth because God's works are perfect. His Words are pure and immutable, and He preserves them from generation to generation forever. All the works of God in the beginning are perfect, true, and complete.

Psalm 119:160

Thy word is true from the BEGINNING: and every one of thy righteous judgments endureth for ever.

Psalm 12:6-7

⁶The words of the LORD are pure words: as silver tried in a furnace of earth, purified seven times. ⁷Thou shalt keep them, O LORD, thou shalt preserve them from this generation for ever.

Matthew 19:3-6

³ The Pharisees also came unto him, tempting him, and saying unto him, Is it lawful for a man to put away his wife for every cause? ⁴ And he answered and said unto them, Have ye not read, that he which made them at the BEGINNING made them male and female, ⁵ And said, For this cause shall a man leave father and mother, and shall cleave to his wife: and they twain shall be one flesh? ⁶ Wherefore they are no more twain, but one flesh. What therefore God hath joined together, let not man put asunder.

1. Half-Naked Dressings:

Just like Jesus, I will as well reference the beginning for authority and truth because the truth of God's Word is immutable. All of God's works in the beginning are perfect, true, and complete. The very first biblical record of clothing is found in Genesis, at the very beginning of all things. A careful biblical analysis of clothing accounts in Genesis and other Scriptures will reveal the nature and purpose of clothing as God intended it.

Genesis 3:5-10,21

5For God doth know that in the day ye eat thereof, then your eyes shall be opened, and ye shall be as gods, knowing good and evil. 6And when the woman saw that the tree was good for food, and that it was pleasant to the eyes, and a tree to be desired to make one wise, she took of the fruit thereof, and did eat, and gave also unto her husband with her; and he did eat. 7And the eyes of them both were opened, and they knew that they were naked; and they sewed fig leaves together, and made themselves aprons. 8And they heard the voice of the LORD God walking in the garden in the cool of the day: and Adam and his wife hid themselves from the presence of the LORD God amongst the trees of the garden. 9And the LORD God called unto Adam, and said unto him, Where art thou? 10And he said, I heard thy voice in the garden, and I was afraid, because I was naked; and I hid myself. 21Unto Adam also and to his wife did the LORD God make coats of skins, and clothed them.

When Adam and Eve sinned against God by eating the fruit of the Tree of the Knowledge of Good and Evil, which He commanded them not to eat. The glory of God, which clothes the saints and Angels, disappeared, and they became naked. Their innocence was gone, now knowing good and evil, they understood that it is not good to be naked. They quickly sewed fig leaves together to make an apron to cover their nakedness. Genesis 3:7, *"And the eyes of them both were opened, and they knew that they were naked; and they sewed fig leaves together, and made themselves aprons."* Nonetheless, the aprons they made were not sufficient to cover their nakedness. An apron is a piece of clothing often tied to the wearer's body to cover some parts of the body. It does not have sufficient material to adequately cover the wearer's body. Does this not describe most of the half-naked dresses that are being peddled to children through these ungodly dolls and celebrities of all kinds? Through these dolls, music artists, TV hosts, sports stars, and influential figures, Satan succeeded in reprogramming the minds of many, including Christians, to accept aprons as clothing. Clothes that could only cover some portions of the breast, back, waist, thighs, and see-through clothing that exposes the body. Christians wear these aprons unashamedly on the streets, to work, and even in the church. Adam and Eve will rise in judgment on the last day to condemn these Christians.

Matthew 12:41

The men of Nineveh shall rise in judgment with this generation, and shall condemn it: because they repented at the preaching of Jonas; and, behold, a greater than Jonas is here.

Adam and Eve will rise in judgment on the last day to condemn these Christians because they were ashamed of wearing aprons. They will condemn those Christians in name only who argue that God only looks at the heart and does not care about the aprons (half-naked dressings) they put on, because they knew in their time that they were still naked despite the aprons. They knew that God cared about their nakedness and were ashamed to stand before God in aprons. They will rise in judgment to condemn them because if they had the technology, materials, and skill set needed to make proper clothing. They would not have unashamedly preferred to make and wear aprons like these Christians in name only. Adam and Eve were ashamed and hid themselves from God because they knew that they were still naked despite the aprons (half-naked clothes) they were wearing.

Genesis 3:7-10

7And the eyes of them both were opened, and they knew that they were naked; and they sewed fig leaves together, and made themselves aprons. 8And they heard the voice of the LORD God walking in the garden in the cool of the day: and Adam and his wife hid themselves from the presence of the LORD God amongst the trees of the garden. 9And the LORD God called unto Adam, and said unto him, Where art thou? 10And he said, I heard thy voice in the garden, and I was afraid, because I was naked; and I hid myself.

God passed great judgment against Adam and Eve for their sin and sent them out of the Garden of Eden. Nonetheless, He made them proper clothing: coats of animal skin to cover their nakedness. Genesis 3:21 ***"Unto Adam also and to his wife did the LORD God make coats of skins, and clothed them."*** If God does not care about the type of clothes His children put on, why then did He make coats to cover their nakedness? Obviously, it was not to reward them because He had just

117

condemned them for their sin. It was not for their luxury and comfort because He had just expelled them from their place of luxury and comfort. What then could it be? It was simply to cover their nakedness. God acknowledged that they were still naked despite the aprons they were wearing, just as Adam rightfully acknowledged their nakedness. Genesis 3:10-11, *"And he said, I heard thy voice in the garden, and I was afraid, because I was naked; and I hid myself. ¹¹And he said, Who told thee that thou wast naked? Hast thou eaten of the tree, whereof I commanded thee that thou shouldest not eat?"*

God, who just judged and condemned Adam and Eve for their sin, was not rewarding them with nice luxury coats of animal skin. That would be confusing and irresponsible on God's part. The primary reason why God made them the coats was to properly cover their nakedness. God wants His children to be properly clothed to cover their nakedness because it is a sin not to do so. God wants His children to adorn themselves with modest clothing with the consciousness of not dressing in a manner that comes across as shameful.

Exodus 28:42-43

⁴²And thou shalt make them linen breeches to cover their nakedness; from the loins even unto the thighs they shall reach: ⁴³And they shall be upon Aaron, and upon his sons, when they come in unto the tabernacle of the congregation, or when they come near unto the altar to minister in the holy place; that they bear not iniquity, and die: it shall be a statute for ever unto him and his seed after him.

God commanded Moses to make breeches (shorts trousers, short pants) for Aaron and his sons to cover their nakedness so that they don't sin against Him. They were to wear the breeches under their coats. Although their coats could completely cover them so that their bodies were not seen. God still required them to wear the breeches underneath to ensure that their body was not exposed in any way. Despite the breeches they wore underneath, God still commanded them not to go up by steps unto His altar so their nakedness would not be exposed. This alone speaks volumes of God's disgust for body exposure.

Leviticus 16:4

He shall put on the holy linen coat, and he shall have the linen breeches upon his flesh, and shall be girded with a linen girdle, and with the linen mitre shall he be attired: these are holy garments; therefore shall he wash his flesh in water, and so put them on.

Exodus 20:26

Neither shalt thou go up by steps unto mine altar, that thy nakedness be not discovered thereon.

The breaches were not made for luxury and glamor to honor Aaron and his sons. Rather, they were made solely to cover their nakedness and keep them from sinning against God with half-naked clothing. These Scriptures clearly reveal God's purpose for making coats for Adam and Eve in Genesis. It was to cover their nakedness and keep them from further sinning against God with their half-naked clothing. God demonstrated to them how to make clothes that would properly cover their nakedness. God is highly interested in the type of clothes His children wear because not being properly covered is a sin against God. These apron-like half-naked dresses being peddled to children through these ungodly dolls, music artists, TV hosts, sports stars, and influential figures are ungodly. Clothes that only cover some portions of the breast, back, waist, thighs, and see-through clothing that exposes the body. Christians should not wear these half-naked clothes because they are sinful and also cause others to sin against God.

Mathew 5:27-28

27Ye have heard that it was said by them of old time, Thou shalt not commit adultery: 28But I say unto you, That whosoever looketh on a woman to lust after her hath committed adultery with her already in his heart.

Romans 14:13

Let us not therefore judge one another any more: but judge this rather, that no man put a stumblingblock or an occasion to fall in his brother's way.

Those who wear these half-naked clothes promote lust in society. Jesus said that a person would be guilty of adultery if he should look at a woman lustfully in his heart, and no adulterer has a place in heaven. Truly, those who wear these half-naked clothes have become agents of Satan, knowingly or unknowingly to them. Their sexually provocative half-nude dresses have caused them to become a stumbling block for many. They are now the tempter of mankind in the likeness of Satan and are causing many to fall. How can they work for Satan and be rewarded by God? Will they send many to hellfire and make it to heaven? Surely, they have no part in the Kingdom of God unless they repent and turn from their wickedness.

2. Jewelry, Hair attachment, Make-up, Fake eyelashes, Fake nails, Hair dyeing, Artificial body parts implants, Tattoos, Bleaching Cream, etc.:

The artificial body parts implants mentioned above are those intended for beauty and not those for medical reasons. There is nothing wrong with replacing a broken tooth or doing plastic surgery to reconstruct a marred body part due to an accident. What I want to address is the use of jewelry, hair attachments, make-up, fake eyelashes, fake nails, hair dyeing, artificial body parts implants, Tattoos, Bleaching Cream, etc., for beautification. When Jesus was called Good Master by the rich young man, He responded that there is none good but God.

Matthew 19:16-17

16And, behold, one came and said unto him, Good Master, what good thing shall I do, that I may have eternal life? 17And he said unto him, Why callest thou me good? there is none good but one, that is, God: but if thou wilt enter into life, keep the commandments.

Jesus made the young man understand that calling Him good is the same as saying that He is God because there is none good but God. This shows the value God places on the word good. However, when God was done with His creation, He said everything He created was very good. God used the adverb "very" to modify/amplify the verb "good" to show the extreme in which His handiworks are perfect and wonderful. The word "good" would have been enough, because it's a word of high value to God which is only ascribed to Him, as Jesus said. Nonetheless, He added "very" to it because they were the works done by the Good God. Therefore, the works came out very good. King David understood this and exclaimed that he was fearfully and wonderfully made by God, and acknowledged that the works of God were marvelous.

Genesis 1:31

And God saw every thing that he had made, and, behold, it was very good. And the evening and the morning were the sixth day.

Psalm 139:14

I will praise thee; for I am fearfully and wonderfully made: marvellous are thy works; and that my soul knoweth right well.

If God had said that His works are very good, and King David, by the Spirit of God, acknowledged that he was fearfully and wonderfully made and that the works of God are marvelous. Why then would anybody want to make up that which is very good? Why would someone in his/her right mind want to alter God's creation that is already made perfect? Why would someone want to add artificial things to beautify or make-up something marvelous, in other words, add something foreign to modify the creation of God that is spectacular, excellent, amazing, and wonderful? The truth is that all these artificial articles of beautification are simply ornaments of innocent disfigurement.

If it were for the disfigurement of that which was fearfully and wonderfully made to be marvelous alone. Then I would not be concerned nor write about it, there would have been no need for alarm. The major issue is that the use of these articles of innocent disfigurement is an unspoken accusation against God that His works are not "very good" as He claimed. It is an unspoken accusation against God that He is a liar. The users of these things are simply saying to God that His works are not very good, without speaking a word. Satan has succeeded in using them to mock and accuse God through their actions. And we know that actions speak louder than words. Their accusations and mockery against God are either true or false. They are either telling the truth by their actions or God is telling the truth; they both can't be correct. And we know what the word of God says concerning this.

Romans 3:3-4

³For what if some did not believe? shall their unbelief make the faith of God without effect? ⁴God forbid: yea, let God be true, but every man a liar; as it is written, That thou mightest be justified in thy sayings, and mightest overcome when thou art judged.

They have become liars themselves through their actions that accuse God of lying and mocking Him, that His works are ugly. They are guilty of lying against God, that His works are not very good as He claimed. Their actions of innocent disfigurement have created false versions of themselves. They are made-up lies, false images of who they really are, and the Bible made it clear that nothing that maketh a lie shall enter the kingdom of God.

Revelation 21:27

And there shall in no wise enter into it any thing that defileth, neither whatsoever worketh abomination, or MAKETH A LIE: but they which are written in the Lamb's book of life.

The use of these ornaments of innocent disfigurement for adornment is the practice of worldly people. God has commanded Christians to separate themselves from the ways of the world and not touch their unclean things. These ornaments of innocent disfigurements like Jewelry, hair attachments, make-up, fake eyelashes, fake nails, hair dyeing, artificial body parts implants, tattoos, bleaching creams, etc., are unclean things. God said He will only be a Father to you when you have separated yourself from the ways of the world and trash those unclean things.

2Corinthians 6:17-18

¹⁷Wherefore come out from among them, and be ye separate, saith the Lord, and touch not the unclean thing; and I will receive you, ¹⁸And will be a Father unto you, and ye shall be my sons and daughters, saith the Lord Almighty.

God said that because of His promises to be a Father to you and give you an inheritance in His Kingdom. You must perfect yourself in holiness by removing all the filthiness of the flesh (Jewelry, hair attachments, make-up, fake eyelashes, fake nails, hair dyeing, artificial body parts implants, tattoos, bleaching cream, etc.), and those of the spirit.

2Corinthians 7:1

Having therefore these promises, dearly beloved, let us cleanse ourselves from all FILTHINESS OF THE FLESH and spirit, perfecting holiness in the fear of God.

These ornaments of innocent disfigurements are defilements and filthiness to the body. True Christian parents must not behave like worldly people in adornment or conduct themselves in the ways they did when they were in ignorance. Their adornments must reflect who they are as Christians. They must adorn themselves in a modest and holy manner, and teach their children the same. The calling of God is unto holiness because He is a holy God. Christians are pilgrims passing through this world. They must keep themselves from the defilements and filthiness of this world in the fear of God. They must do this and teach their children the same if they desire to make it to heaven with their family to be with God forever.

1Peter 1:14-17

[14]As obedient children, not fashioning yourselves according to the former lusts in your ignorance: [15]But as he which hath called you is holy, so be ye holy in all manner of conversation; [16]Because it is written, Be ye holy; for I am holy. [17]And if ye call on the Father, who without respect of persons judgeth according to every man's work, pass the time of your sojourning here in fear:

5.6 Demonic Possession Through Cartoons, Video Games, and Dolls

Since the emergence of cartoon films over a century ago, several generations of children have grown up watching animated movies. Many girls have fantasized about being princesses, and many boys have imagined themselves to be valiant knights after watching cartoons like Peter Pan, Aladdin and the Magic Lamp, Cinderella, Beauty and the Beast, etc. Why do children want to become these cartoon characters, and why do they manifest the ungodly behaviors of these cartoon and video game characters?

Most of these cartoons and video game characters are facsimiles of demonic spirits. This is why you find that in recent times, cartoon characters have become monstrous and are all kinds of creepy and scary creatures. Have you ever wondered why the sudden change of cartoon characters to monstrous images? Are scary images the best appeal to children? Satan has been animating demons, giving them charming and charismatic characters and presenting them to children as adorable heroes.

These demonic spirits present themselves as heroes with loving and charming charismatic characters worthy of idolizing.

2Corinthians 11:14-15

¹⁴And no marvel; for Satan himself is transformed into an angel of light. ¹⁵Therefore it is no great thing if his ministers also be transformed as the ministers of righteousness; whose end shall be according to their works.

Satan is very subtle; deception and manipulation are his strongest weapons to kill, steal, and destroy as recorded in John 10:10. Demons are his ministers. They are his ministering spirits. He has transformed many of his demons into ministers of righteousness to deceive Christians through false revelations. In the same way, Satan has also transformed these demons into animated heroes of charming and adorable charismatic characters to deceive children. Most of these cartoon characters, including the good-looking and the monstrous ones, are facsimiles of demonic spirits. This is evident by the ungodly character and attitude they display and glamorize to the children. Character such as bratty behavior, lying, tantrums, stubbornness, rebellion, violence, immoral sexual behaviors, etc. The children are deceived, and they fall in love with these demonic replicas and deem them friendly. Then they start to idolize and imitate the characters of these demonic animated characters.

The children are desensitized from fearing these would have been scary images because of their heroic and charming characters. These demonic spirits then appear to the children in the dream as their familiar dolls, cartoons, and game characters to possess them. Now, because the children have been desensitized and deceived into seeing them as friendly and charismatic, they will not be alarmed. The children will freely embrace and interact with them, and these demons will enter them, and they will become possessed. This is why you see some children uncontrollably manifest some of these ungodly characteristics like tantrums, lying, stubbornness, rebellion, sexual immorality, anger, violence, etc., at levels beyond human comprehension. You would have also observed that every effort made to help and change children like this is usually fruitless. This is because the matter has gone beyond the physical; the matter is spiritual, and only Jesus can deliver them.

It is satanic manipulation and deception to make parents think that their children would not have a normal childhood and grow into responsible, functional adults without these dolls and other kiddifying devices. I always want to examine matters from the empirical standpoint; that is, from the point of experience and observations. Many generations grew up without these Satan's kiddifying devices. Could anyone say that they did not have a normal childhood, or say that they did not become responsible and functional adults? You may not have grown up with these kiddifying devices. Would you claim to be dysfunctional in life because you were not raised with these things? Could anyone say that the generations that grew up without these kiddifying devices are more morally bankrupt? The answers to these questions are obvious. On the contrary, it is the generations that grew up with these satanic kiddifying agents that are more morally bankrupt and dysfunctional because they were Kiddified.

Don't 'Kiddify' your children, is simply saying, don't hand over your children to Satan through his kiddifying devices like TV, social media, music, cartoons, dolls, video games, and other Satanic kiddifying devices. Satan is a goat-like spirit being, filled with rebellion and stubbornness towards God. For this reason, the image of Satan is represented by a goat-like anthropomorphic creature; the Baphomet image. If you leave your children in his hands, he will raise them up goat-like spirited children in his likeness. Children who have been Kiddified, filled with rebellion, stubbornness, and all manner of sinfulness. Untrained children who will not come to the LORD nor obey Him. Children whom the LORD will not recognize. Children who will end up with their father, Satan, in hellfire for all eternity.

Matthew 25:33-34, 41

³³And he shall set the sheep on his right hand, but the goats on the left. ³⁴Then shall the King say unto them on his right hand, Come, ye blessed of my Father, inherit the kingdom prepared for you from the foundation of the world: ⁴¹Then shall he say also unto them on the left hand, Depart from me, ye cursed, into everlasting fire, prepared for the devil and his angels:

5.7 Recommendations and Alternatives to Cartoons, Video Games, and Dolls

All that has been discussed previously is not to say that one should not buy any type of toy, doll, or video game, or allow their children to watch any type of cartoon. All that I have pointed out is that the devil uses these things to devise mischief for the children. Also, these things are unnecessary in raising a child to become a moral and functional adult. Therefore, parents must exercise knowledge, wisdom, and great caution in buying and in what they allow their children to watch. Christian parents must guard against Satan from kiddifying their children with these devices. That is to say, guard against Satan from turning your children into spiritual goats through cartoons, video games, and dolls. This being said, the most important thing is that they should not become an alternative to parenting. They should not replace parental roles in their children's lives. They must not take the most important part of your children's lives. Parents must sacrifice time to be there to nurture and train their children if they truly want to raise godly children. They must transform their children's lives with the Word of God.

Romans 12:2

And be not conformed to this world: but be ye transformed by the renewing of your mind, that ye may prove what is that good, and acceptable, and perfect, will of God.

Christian parents should devise fun ways to keep their children busy with the Word of God and should be involved. This will keep the children from conforming to the ways of the world and the desires of the world. This is why Romans 12:2 further admonishes us to become transformed from this world's system of thought and sinful lifestyles by renewing our minds with the Word of God. This will invariably produce the heavenly system of thoughts that will produce the desired godly lifestyle.

Recommendations:

1. Parents should not use cartoons and video games as their babysitters.
2. Parents should avoid all cartoons and video games for entertainment if possible.
3. Avoid educational cartoons where possible and use children's educational videos taught by actual humans.

4. Allow only appropriate educational cartoons where necessary if inevitable.
5. Limit the time spent watching inevitable necessary educational cartoons.
6. Parents should watch TV/cartoons with their children and always take time to explain the difference between cartoons and reality as the need arises.
7. Parents should not allow their children to eat with the TV or iPad on.
8. Parents should not leave their children with TV or iPad alone for long without monitoring them.

Alternatives to Cartoons and Video Games:

1. Children love outside games (Jump rope, running, soccer, etc.). Children will forget that TV, iPads, Phones, and dolls exist once they are outside. The problem is that most parents have sold and enslaved themselves to dollars. Therefore, they have no time to sacrifice for their children to do the things that children actually love doing. Most of these devices are usually relevant only when children cannot go out to play.
2. Instead of going to the gym and spending unnecessary money. Turn your workout time into time with the children outside. Engaging with the children in outside games will burn the calories needed and simultaneously create quality time with the children, eliminating the need for any kiddifying device.
3. Create Bible story time and have your children tell the Bible stories, and the family can ask them questions. This presupposes that parents have already created the

environment for their children to learn the Bible. Otherwise, how could they be able to tell Bible stories? Christian parents must teach their children the Word of God that is able to transform them.

4. Organize family Bible quizzes with rewards. Set a long-term prize reward like quarterly, six months, and yearly, and keep records of scores to build up for the prizes. Please let the prizes or rewards not be the same things you are trying to get them away from (iPads, games, phones, dolls, etc.)

5. **Your turn to add to the list...**

CHAPTER 6

Thou Shall Not Spare the Rod

You could raise a child with great decorum, that is, a child with dignified behavior, speech, and orderliness as expected in polite or civil society, without the rod of correction. However, you may not be able to raise a child with godly fear that will produce in him or her the holiness required for heaven without the rod of correction. The rod of correction is any stick that can be safely and reasonably used to beat a child to discipline and correct him or her without harming the child. That is what the Bible says in Proverbs 23:13: "***Withhold not correction from the child: for if thou beatest him with the rod, he shall not die.***" The rod of correction is an essential tool for raising godly children for the LORD. The LORD prescribed it Himself because of its importance in raising godly children for Him. Nonetheless, there is a great difference between physically abusing a child and disciplining a child with the rod of correction.

Proverbs 23:13-14

¹³Withhold not correction from the child: for if thou beatest him with the rod, he shall not die. ¹⁴Thou shalt beat him with the rod, and shalt deliver his soul from hell.

One of Satan's milestone achievements is convincing parents that disciplining their children with the rod of correction when necessary is child abuse. Satan, through his various agents, convinced the world that the pain inflicted with the rod of correction is evil and amounts to child abuse. He made humanity see any sort of pain or sorrow as evil and of no value to human development and safety. The use of the rod of correction on children is a godly act because it was God who prescribed its use. The rod of correction produces godly sorrow that leads a child to repent of his evil ways. Its use is something meant to be done with a loving intention to save children from destructive characters. It is not to be done in cruelty or wickedness against a child, which will produce destructive worldly sorrows. Its use is aimed at producing godly sorrow and fear. Christian parents should not be apologetic, feel bad, or be intimidated for using it.

2Corrinthians 7:10

For godly sorrow worketh repentance to salvation not to be repented of: but the sorrow of the world worketh death.

Pain and the ability to feel pain are necessary for healthy physical and spiritual human development and safety. A healthy person with the ability to feel pain may not value this ability until he or she meets a person with CIPA (Congenital Insensitivity to Pain with Anhidrosis). CIPA is a rare genetic disorder that prevents the development of nerve cells that transmit pain and temperature signals to the brain. A person suffering from this disorder cannot feel pain. He or she could step on a sharp object like a nail or place a hand on a hot stove and not feel any pain. Imagine having to raise a child like this, who could unknowingly harm or kill himself with a dangerous object or burn to death because of the inability to feel pain. You will pray day and night, pleading with God to give your child the ability to feel pain. You would give anything just for that child to be able to feel pain. Then you will value the ability to feel pain and fully understand the importance of pain in human development and safety. God in His infinite wisdom engineered the ability to feel pain in the human body and commanded parents to take advantage of it in raising godly children for Him.

Proverbs 22:15

Foolishness is bound in the heart of a child; but the rod of correction shall drive it far from him.

Proverbs 19:18

Chasten thy son while there is hope, and let not thy soul spare for his crying.

Proverbs 13:24

He that spareth his rod hateth his son: but he that loveth him chasteneth him betimes.

Proverbs 23:13-14

[13]Withhold not correction from the child: for if thou beatest him with the rod, he shall not die. [14]Thou shalt beat him with the rod, and shalt deliver his soul from hell.

Notwithstanding, Satan was still able to convince humanity not to utilize this asset that God engineered in the human body to raise physically and spiritually healthy children. Unfortunately, many churches and Christians were also deceived into believing Satan that the rod of correction is evil, contrary to the Word of God. Then Satan used the government to pass laws that prohibit parents from using the rod of correction on their children. Remember points 2 and 10 of the Satanic 10 points agenda by the infamous Satanist Alice A Bailey.

2. REDUCE PARENTAL AUTHORITY OVER THE CHILDREN.

10. GET GOVERNMENTS TO MAKE ALL THESE LAWS AND GET THE CHURCH TO ENDORSE THESE CHANGES.

Unfortunately, many churches have endorsed these satanic legislations that demonize the use of the rod of correction in raising godly children. Many Christian parents have abandoned disciplining their children with the rod of correction either because they bought the lies of the devil or for fear of the government. Since most of the Western world became civilized above God's Word and entered the bed with the devil by doing away with the rod of correction. How has their generation turned out? Have the children brought up without the rod of correction turned out to be more morally upright and grown into morally upright adults? All you have to do is look around you at home, watch or listen to the news, look at the social media, look at the schools, look everywhere. What can you observe, and what have you experienced? Then, let empiricism deliver an unbiased, unequivocal answer to you.

Romans 3: 4

God forbid: yea, let God be true, but every man a liar; as it is written, That thou mightest be justified in thy sayings, and mightest overcome when thou art judged.

The Bible says, "Let God be true, but every man a liar, that God may be justified in His sayings when He is Judged." Man under the influence of Satan for many generations has often judged God's Word to be irrelevant, and the effect has consistently been catastrophic for man. It all started in the

Garden of Eden; it was the despising of God's Word by Eve and Adam as influenced by Satan that led to their eating of the Tree of Good and Evil Genesis 2:15-17; 3:1-7. Since then, man has continued to reap the resulting catastrophic consequences to date. Nonetheless, man has not learned to trust God's Word with his whole heart even when he does not fully understand why it was said. God spoke unequivocally in the Bible about the use of the rod of correction in training children. Nevertheless, many claim it is unclear and irrelevant, and has deliberately misinterpreted them to fit their narrative and choice.

Despite the clarity of God's Word on the use of the rod of correction. Christian parents, just like Adam and Eve, have despised God's Word in using this essential tool for training godly children. Consequently, they are reaping their catastrophic harvest in abundance. Why? So that God may be justified in His sayings when He is judged by man. Many pastors and teachers have craftily explained away the use of the rod of correction, either because they are not true ministers of the gospel, or because they are afraid. Chastening is to inflict suffering upon a person for the purpose of moral improvement. If it does not imply pain, why then is the LORD saying that you should not mind their crying? Proverbs 19:18 ***"Chasten thy son while there is hope, and let not thy soul spare for his crying."*** That pain will lead to godly sorrow that will compel the child to repent from his or her evil character. The rod of correction is any stick/object that can be safely and reasonably used to beat a child to discipline and correct him without harming the child. That is what the Bible says in Proverbs 23:13 ***"Withhold not correction from the child: for if thou beatest him with the rod, he shall not die."*** Remember, you could raise a child with great decorum without the rod of correction. However, you may not be able to raise a child with the godly fear that will produce the holiness required for heaven without the rod of correction. Proverbs 23:14, *"Thou shalt beat him with the rod, and shalt deliver his soul from hell."*

6.1 Introduce the Rod of Correction at Ground-Zero.

You cannot afford to toy with your children at the ground-zero stage of their life, that is, age zero. This is the foundation of the child; whatever you want to achieve in your child must start here. If you want to raise a godly child with great decorum, it must start here. All training must start at Ground-Zero for effectiveness, and this includes the use of the rod of correction. The rod of correction is most effective when used early. Remember early childhood psychology: "The earlier the better." The issue of abuse mostly comes in when parents fail to discipline their children promptly from Ground-Zero. When parents fail to bring up their children to fear and respect them from Ground-Zero. Then they will later start trying to demand respect and obedience from the children who were never trained to fear and respect them. Parents must start training their children from Ground-Zero to have a healthy reverential fear for them. Just like the kind of fear a good citizen would have for the police officer. Your children should be able to fear you enough not to do wrong because of the consequences that may arise through you. Whatever you fail to impart to your children at the foundational stage will cost you a great deal in the future.

Proverbs 19:18

Chasten thy son while there is hope, and let not thy soul spare for his crying.

There is a window of hope in chastening children with the rod of correction. This window opens at Ground-Zero and continues to close with each passing day. This is why the Bible says that you should chasten your children without minding their crying while there is hope. This implies that there will be a time when all hope of ever achieving anything in their life through chastening will be completely lost. Most parents think that pampering and playing with their children is all there is to loving them. Many parents profess to love their children, and all they labor for every day is just to make their children laugh and merry. They deny their children the rod of correction because they don't want to see them cry; poor child, your mother hates you. The truth is, denying your children the rod of correction necessary for their godly development when needed actually shows you hate them. Parents who truly love their children are the ones who chastise them promptly with the rod of correction when necessary.

Proverbs 13:24

He that spareth his rod hateth his son: but he that loveth him chasteneth him betimes.

Hebrews 12:6-8

⁶For whom the Lord loveth he chasteneth, and scourgeth every son whom he receiveth. ⁷If ye endure chastening, God dealeth with you as with sons; for what son is he whom the father chasteneth not? ⁸But if ye be without chastisement, whereof all are partakers, then are ye bastards, and not sons.

The Almighty God, who is love personified, says that He chastens and scourges the son He loves. God further asked, "What son is he whom the father chasteneth not?" Then He said that those without chastening are bastards. Chastening is to inflict suffering upon a person for the purpose of moral improvement. This is the Almighty God speaking; anyone who tells you otherwise is a messenger of Satan. Any pastor who tells you that chastening your child with the rod of correction, as written in the Bible, does not literally mean what it says. That pastor is just a philosopher from hell. Then how can you claim to love your children and deny them the love of chastening them with the rod of correction when necessary? If you start early enough to chasten your children promptly with the rod of correction, you will have rest as they grow. The chastening with the rod of correction you gave them early while the window of chastening was still open will give you rest in their later years.

Proverbs 29:17

Correct thy son, and he shall give thee rest; yea, he shall give delight unto thy soul.

Remember my story on disciplining a friend's child from Ground-Zero that I narrated in chapter two? That child grew up with reverential fear for me because of the little spanks I gave her on her fingers from Ground-Zero as she was growing up. Then, when she was around five/six years old, I never had any need to use the rod of correction on her because she had grown up with reverential fear for me. Mostly, all I needed at any point in time was to tell her what she should do or not do, and she would be diligent to obey because she understands that there would be consequences. Then on the other side, her mother, who did not start disciplining her from Ground-Zero, is now physically abusing her at about this same age. Why? Because she grew up without the fear of consequences from her mother, and now, out of frustration and anger, she wants to enforce obedience. The resulting act is usually physically abusive because the mother will always go into a reckless beating of the child with her hands out of anger and frustration. If she had started early at Ground-Zero to apply the rod of correction, the child would have grown up with a reverential fear for her. This would have saved her from the headaches, anger, and frustration, and saved the child from physical abuse.

Hebrews 12:11

Now no chastening for the present seemeth to be joyous, but grievous: nevertheless afterward it yieldeth the peaceable fruit of righteousness unto them which are exercised thereby.

6.2 The Difference Between Abusing and Disciplining Children

Discipline your children according to God's Word with the rod of correction and do not abuse them physically. Any good parent will know when they have pushed the button too far and have abused their children instead of correcting them. Physical abuse is most likely to occur when parents beat their children out of anger in the heat of the moment. At that moment of anger, they will use anything they can lay their hands on to afflict the child. Some will even throw shoes or anything they can lay their hands on at the child because of anger. Some will use their hands to slap, punch, and hit the child from any direction possible, not minding what part of the body they hit. Treating your children this way is physical abuse and not the discipline of the rod of correction the Bible recommends. It is foolishness on the side of the parent; Ecclesiastes 7:9, **"Be not hasty in thy spirit to be angry: for anger resteth in the bosom of fools."** Parents must control and overcome anger before beating their children with the rod of correction. This may sometimes require parents to wait until they are fully in control of their emotions. Then they can call the child to be disciplined and fully let him or her know what they did wrong and why you have prescribed X amount of the rod of correction for their discipline.

Parents are like doctors when it comes to disciplining their children with the rod of correction. Imagine going to see your doctor feeling healthy just for a checkup. Then your doctor gives you a bag of medications, orders you to be given an injection, or sends you to the operating table, without telling you what was wrong with you. You will surely object to that treatment no matter what illness the doctor is trying to arrest and demand to know what is wrong with you. In the same vein, children will also resist the correction you are aiming to achieve with the rod of correction if you do not take time to make them understand what they have done wrong. They may not verbally speak, but in their heart, they will be offended and angry with you instead of being truly remorseful for their wrong.

Ephesians 6:4

And, ye fathers, provoke not your children to wrath: but bring them up in the nurture and admonition of the Lord.

Just like the doctor applies thought to the circumstance of his patient and considers the data available and the history of the patient, and the illness in order to prescribe the right treatment. In the same way, parents must be rational and consider the mental data available on their children's behavior. Consider the history and the gravity of the offense committed to rightfully prescribe the right discipline. I said discipline and not the rod of correction because it is not in all cases that the rod of correction should be prescribed. The doctor does not always prescribe the injection or operation for every illness; some just require medication. Parents should know that sometimes all that is required is to sit with a child and educate them to understand what they did wrong and the consequences. The doctor's aim in prescribing any treatment is to cure and deliver his patient from sickness and not to punish his patient. The parents' aim in prescribing the rod of correction should also be to cure and deliver their children from evil character and not to punish them. When the rod of correction is used appropriately, the child will accept the correction in his or her heart, and discipline will be achieved.

6.3 The Rod of Correction Drives Away Foolishness

Children are a bundle of joy to their parents. Nonetheless, as revealed in the Scripture, they are mischievous by nature and empirically certified to be true. It is natural for children to want to do foolish things because foolishness is in their hearts. But God said that the rod of correction will drive that foolishness far away from them. Let God be true and every man a liar.

Proverbs 22:15

Foolishness is bound in the heart of a child; but the rod of correction shall drive it far from him.

Anyone who has a child, or was once a child of which everyone once was, knows with all certainty that foolishness is bound in the heart of a child. As a parent, you would have observed your children do things that made you wonder and say, "What foolishness!" As an adult, there are some things you did as a child that when you remember them, you would say, "How foolish was I, what was I thinking?" Empirically, that is, based on observation and experience, everyone would agree with the Word of God that foolishness is bound in the heart of a child. Therefore, if the first part of Proverbs 22:15 could be empirically certified by all, then the second part of that verse should also be empirically certified by all. Why then are some people denying the validity of this verse and attempting to metaphorically explain it away? The devil is in the details.

I am a typical example of one whose parents' rod of correction drove plenty of foolishness away from his life. Growing up, a lot of foolishness was bound in my heart, but my parents' rod of correction drove them very far away from me. I had two no-nonsense condoning parents who were blessed with seven children. Our father and mother did not spare their rod of correction on us. They disciplined us promptly with the rod of correction whenever necessary, not because they hated us but because they loved us and wanted us to turn out responsible adults. Proverbs 13:24 ***"He that spareth his rod hateth his son: but he that loveth him chasteneth him betimes."*** We had parents who loved us so much and gave us the best of everything in life they could afford. They gave us the best of education, clothing, food, medical care, protection, and also the best of the rod of correction. All these they did because they loved us with their whole heart. Growing up, a lot of foolishness was bound in

143

my heart and those of my siblings, but our parents' rod of correction worked wonders in driving them very far away from us. I could only imagine what most of us would have turned out to be without our parents' rod of correction. But to the glory of God, we all turned out to become responsible God-fearing law-abiding citizens wherever we've all found ourselves on the face of the earth. And just like the Bible says in Proverbs 23:13, *"**Withhold not correction from the child: for if thou beatest him with the rod, he shall not die.**"* Yes, we did not die from their beatings; we are still alive and living a good life. None of us is negatively affected physically, psychologically, or emotionally as some devil's advocates would claim that disciplining children with the rod of correction does. Rather, our parents' rod of correction was instrumental in driving foolishness away from us and helped train us to become responsible godly children. Let God be true and all men liars!

Romans 3: 4

God forbid: yea, let God be true, but every man a liar; as it is written, That thou mightest be justified in thy sayings, and mightest overcome when thou art judged.

6.4 The Rod of Correction Delivers from Hell

The propensity to deliver a person from hell is the most important benefit of the rod of correction. You could raise a child with dignified behavior, speech, and orderliness as expected in polite or civil society without the rod of correction. However, you may not be able to raise a child with godly fear that will produce in him or her the holiness required for heaven without the rod of correction. The point here is that raising a godly heaven-bound child without the rod of correction is almost impossible, if not impossible. There is a natural inclination derived from the rod of correction that gives an understanding of judgment, and painful consequences that tend to deliver a person from hell. Pain and the ability to feel pain are necessary for healthy physical and spiritual human development and safety. The ability to feel pain and the understanding that a hot stove would cause pain will keep an individual away from such an object. A healthy person capable of feeling pain may take this ability for granted. However, parents of a child with CIPA (Congenital Insensitivity to Pain with Anhidrosis) fully understand the necessity of pain and the ability to feel pain in raising a child. A child with CIPA could step on a sharp object like a nail or place a hand on a hot stove and not feel any pain. The child is insensitive to pain and has no understanding of painful consequences to help him move away from painful and destructive objects. The same is a child trained without the rod of correction. That child may have decorum, but may not understand how eternal, painful consequences in hell could come from the loving God as a result of sin. Because his earthly parents never used the rod of correction to teach him that painful consequences could come from loving parents because of bad behaviors.

Proverbs 23:13-14

13Withhold not correction from the child: for if thou beatest him with the rod, he shall not die. 14Thou shalt beat him with the rod, and shalt deliver his soul from hell.

God said you shall beat your child with the rod of correction and deliver his soul from hell. Note that God did not say, "him" but, "his soul." This shows that God was emphatically speaking of eternal hell because flesh and blood do not go to hell, but the souls of men. This is the main reason Satan has worked so hard against the application of this scripture and largely has succeeded, especially in the Western world. Satan used the government to create all kinds of excessive rights and laws to hinder children from being delivered from hell. Claiming that it is physical abuse when a child is disciplined with the rod of correction. Unfortunately, the church endorsed it, and Christian parents have agreed with the devil. If God had said that you should beat your children with the rod of correction to deliver their souls from hell, then you should not wonder who is behind stopping the use of it. Satan is a thief who opposes God's Word in all areas of life because he wants to steal, kill, and destroy all humans and damn their souls in hell. Satan's agenda was unequivocally revealed by our Lord and Savior Jesus Christ in the Scripture.

Jonh 10:10

The thief cometh not, but for to steal, and to kill, and to destroy: I am come that they might have life, and that they might have it more abundantly.

Let me give you an understanding of why it is almost impossible for people raised without the rod of correction to make heaven. Children raised without the rod of correction grow up without experiencing any painful consequences for their wrong actions. You might say, I deprived them of their phone, I gave them a timeout, etc. Those are simply momentary deprivations of pleasure time and are good forms of discipline when used at the appropriate time. However, depriving children of these things inflicts no pain for wrongdoings but only a momentary loss of pleasure time. Parents should know that the advocacy by the world, government, and unbelieving believers to replace the use of the rod of correction with momentary deprivation of pleasure time is Satan's subtle deception to stop parents from delivering their children's souls from hell. Children raised without the rod of correction see their parents as very loving for all the wrong reasons. They see them as loving parents because they let them get away with stuff. The worst they would ever do is to put them in timeout or deprive them of their iPads, phones, video games, etc. They are so loving that they would never inflict pain on them with the rod of correction. Those children will become adults without ever experiencing pain from their parents as a direct consequence of their wrongdoings. Now remember that God is also a Parent; He is a Father to those who believe in Him.

John 1:12-13

12But as many as received him, to them gave he power to become the sons of God, even to them that believe on his name: 13Which were born, not of blood, nor of the will of the flesh, nor of the will of man, but of God.

2Corinthians 6:17-18

17Wherefore come out from among them, and be ye separate, saith the Lord, and touch not the unclean thing; and I will receive you, 18And will be a Father unto you, and ye shall be my sons and daughters, saith the Lord Almighty.

Second Corinthians 2:17-18 says that for God to be a Father to anyone, they have to separate themselves from the world's philosophies and ways of thinking. The world's reasoning, which is Satan's, is that you should not discipline your child with the rod of correction. God is saying, you should not conform to the world's ways of thinking and doing things. God wants Christians to renew their mind with His Word so that they will be able to discern what is right and acceptable and know His perfect will for them and their children.

Romans 12:2

And be not conformed to this world: but be ye transformed by the renewing of your mind, that ye may prove what is that good, and acceptable, and perfect, will of God.

God's will on the use of the rod of correction as stated in the Scripture is clear enough for babes to understand. If it is so clear, why then is there so much confusion on the use of the rod of correction? Satan is in the details; he is the author of confusion; he wants to turn good to be perceived as evil and evil to be perceived as good. He has turned the good, godly practice of disciplining children with the rod of correction to be perceived as evil. And has turned the ungodly practice of not disciplining children with the rod of correction to be perceived and accepted as good. Many people have been raised in the world today and are still being raised without the rod of correction. The effect of this kind of upbringing is that when such children hear true teachings on God's judgment and eternal punishment in hell for sin, they cannot comprehend it. Especially for what they would term as a little sin. Things that their parent did not give them any type of discipline for doing, nor inflict pain on them with the rod of correction. Then when they hear that God will damn a person in hell for all eternity for things their parents laughed over. That the loving God would put His children in hell for all eternity for just lying. They will not be able to comprehend that a loving God would ever inflict such eternal pain and suffering on His children. Notwithstanding that, it is boldly written all over the Scripture.

Revelation 21:7-8

⁷He that overcometh shall inherit all things; and I will be his God, and he shall be my son. ⁸But the fearful, and unbelieving, and the abominable, and murderers, and whoremongers, and sorcerers, and idolaters, and all liars, shall have their part in the lake which burneth with fire and brimstone: which is the second death.

Psalm 9:16-17

¹⁶The LORD is known by the judgment which he executeth: the wicked (Sinner) is snared in the work of his own hands. ¹⁷The wicked (Sinner) shall be turned into hell, and all the nations that forget God.

Isaiah 66:24

And they shall go forth, and look upon the carcases of the men that have transgressed against me: for their worm shall not die, neither shall their fire be quenched; and they shall be an abhorring unto all flesh.

Then Satan will inspire them to compare God with their earthly father. They will reason thus: if my father, a human being, can be so loving to me, that is, never inflicted any kind of pain on me, no matter what I did). Then why would God, who is said to be a good God and Father, send anyone to hell? Then Satan will remind them of all the terrible, no-good, mischievous things they did growing up and only got a timeout or were deprived of using their gadgets for a while. With the help of Satan, they will not believe that God would ever damn His children in hell.

149

Especially for things like lying, forgetting God, or any other thing, for that matter, because God is love. This will create great confusion in their mind and consequently rebellion against God. This is why you find many adults of great decorum, of high and low status in society, even professing Christians, lying without fear of eternal consequences. Pastors, presidents, senators, CEOs, lawyers, judges, teachers, and parents of dignified behavior, speech, and orderliness as expected in a civil society all lie without the fear of God's judgment. This is the reason why many Christian sects do not believe in hell despite it being unequivocally spoken of by Jesus Christ. They outrightly reject the existence of hell despite it being written across the Scripture from the Old Testament to the New Testament. They philosophically explain hell away because they cannot imagine a loving God ever putting His children through such a horrific ordeal for all eternity. This is the reason why the doctrine of eternal security of salvation was able to spread like cancer across the Western world, and is still spreading to the entire world. These are the kind of doctrines people raised without the rod of correction would most likely accept. Doctrines of demons that tend to diminish the weight or severity of God's Word. Doctrines that misinterpret the Word of God and present false benefits to keep their hearers unperturbed in their sins. Doctrines that make light of the seriousness of God's Word and the severe eternal consequences of disobeying them.

Satan is very strategic; all these were in his plan when he pushed for the abolition of the use of the rod of correction. Now the churches are filled with hell-bound believers who believe that God is just a sweet, loving Father like their earthly fathers who never disciplined them with the rod of correction. Therefore, He will never inflict them with the eternal pain and sorrow of hellfire. People who believe that they are God's children and will never go to hell, no matter how much sin they commit in disobedience and rebellion against God. Why do they believe this? because they have accepted Jesus as their Lord and Savior whom they do not obey. Certainly, Jesus is not their Lord because they do not obey Him. Luke 6:46, *"And why call ye me, Lord, Lord, and do not the things which I say?"* They fear no consequences of hell because God is a sweet, loving Father and will never inflict them with such terrible pain in hell, just like they got no painful consequences for disobeying their earthly parents. Even when people like this are members of a holy ministry like Jesus' End-Time Ministry, Holiness Revival Movement Worldwide. A place where the complete truth and doctrines of God's Word are taught in the power of the Holy Ghost. They will still find it very difficult to truly fear God and obey Him in their private lives. They may continue to toy with what they might term as little sins like lying, malice, etc., because it is hard for them to fully comprehend how their loving Father would not pardon them for such little sins. They would struggle to understand the strictness and impartiality of God in judgment because of their upbringing. The lack of the rod of correction in their upbringing, which formed the foundation of their lives, drives their worldview on matters of consequences for wrongdoings. They will liken the Almighty Father to their earthly father who never inflicted any pain on them in discipline, thereby putting them in danger of the everlasting wrath of God in hell.

When children are appropriately disciplined with the rod of correction, and experience pain from a loving parent. They will understand that it was for their good that their loving parent had to inflict pain on them to discipline them because of their bad behavior. Such children grow up with an understanding that a loving father could inflict pain on his children for their disobedience and wrongdoings. Intuitively, they will understand God's judgment and eternal consequences for sin and disobedience against Him as the Bible reveals. People trained with the rod of correction most likely will not have a problem understanding that a loving Father like God could put His children in the pain and sorrow of hell for sin, disobedience, and rebellion. They most likely will not have a problem accepting sound biblical doctrines that can deliver them from God's eternal punishment in hell. They would be able to relate to God according to the truth of His Word. They would easily understand that a loving God could inflict pain on them for doing evil, just like their earthly father, who loved them, did inflict pain on them for doing evil. It will not be difficult for them to understand the strictness and impartiality of God in judgment. Romans 2:11, *"For there is no respect of persons with God."* People raised with the rod of correction are most likely to have a healthy fear of God, His judgment, and the eternal consequences of sin in hell. Let God be true and all men liars!

Romans 3: 4

God forbid: yea, let God be true, but every man a liar; as it is written, That thou mightest be justified in thy sayings, and mightest overcome when thou art judged.

Proverbs 23:13-14

13Withhold not correction from the child: for if thou beatest him with the rod, he shall not die. 14Thou shalt beat him with the rod, and shalt deliver his soul from hell.

CHAPTER 7

Thou Shall Not Spare the Word

The word here is the Word of God. Thou shall not spare the Word of God if you want to raise a godly child for the LORD. The Word of God is the building block for raising a godly child. You must build your children's foundation with the building blocks of God's Word. All human effort to train children can only do so much. It is the Word of God that brings true and lasting change in children. It is only God's Word that has the power to transform a mischievous child into a godly child. For the young man (youth) to be able to hide the Word of God in his heart and stay away from sin, someone has to lay the foundation of his life with God's Word. It is the parents' responsibility to hide the Word of God in their children's hearts at the foundational stage. Children at the foundational age will accept whatever you give them. They will believe whatever you tell them. At ages zero to seven, they have not started making discoveries of their own and forming their own opinions. They have not started to discover the truth on their own and have no mind of their own, but completely rely on their parents for all guidance in the knowledge of the truth. Therefore, they will accept whatever knowledge you want to implant in them. Whatever knowledge you impart to them at that stage will form the foundation of their life, which will most likely last a lifetime. What better knowledge could parents who want to raise godly children impart, if not the Word of God? The Word of God produces the godly fear that will keep your children from straying tomorrow. Jedidiah did that for Josiah; Eunice and her mother Lois, did the same for Timothy, Paul's protégé. The Word of God is the true nourishment that children need to grow into healthy, godly adults.

2 Timothy 1:5-6

When I call to remembrance the unfeigned faith that is in thee, which dwelt first in thy grandmother Lois, and thy mother Eunice; and I am persuaded that in thee also.

Psalm 119:9-11

⁹Wherewithal shall a young man cleanse his way? by taking heed thereto according to thy word. ¹⁰With my whole heart have I sought thee: O let me not wander from thy commandments. ¹¹Thy word have I hid in mine heart, that I might not sin against thee.

Luke 4:4

And Jesus answered him, saying, It is written, That man shall not live by bread alone, but by every word of God.

John 6:26

Jesus answered them and said, Verily, verily, I say unto you, Ye seek me, not because ye saw the miracles, but because ye did eat of the loaves, and were filled.

Man shall not live by bread alone means that man will die eternally if all he feeds on is earthly food. Satan understands that the Word of God is the building block for a person's life. He knows that man shall not live by bread alone. He will do anything he possibly can to stop parents from building their children's lives with this life-giving nourishment. This is why he deceived parents to occupy their children with all his kiddifying devices at their foundational stage. His sole aim is to ensure that the children grow up without adequate knowledge of the Word of God. Satan knows that nothing destroys a person, family, and nation like the lack of knowledge. That is the knowledge of the Word of God.

Hosea 4:1,6

⁴Hear the word of the LORD, ye children of Israel: for the LORD hath a controversy with the inhabitants of the land, because there is no truth, nor mercy, NOR KNOWLEDGE OF GOD IN THE LAND. ⁶MY PEOPLE ARE DESTROYED FOR LACK OF KNOWLEDGE: because thou hast rejected knowledge, I will also reject thee, that thou shalt be no priest to me: SEEING THOU HAST FORGOTTEN THE LAW OF THY GOD, I WILL ALSO FORGET THY CHILDREN.

7.1 God's Word Gives Light and Understanding to the Simple

Psalm 119:130

The entrance of thy words giveth light; it giveth understanding unto the simple.

God said that the entrance of His words gives light and understanding to the simple. Light, as used in this Bible verse, means understood knowledge. Someone could have knowledge but yet lack the understanding of what he knows. Knowledge with understanding illuminates the darkness of ignorance in the simple. When someone receives the knowledge of God's Word, they will gain understanding and be illuminated by the light of God's Word; they become wise. The simple refers to the simple-hearted. A child is a perfect example of one whose heart is simple. This is why Jesus said that except one becomes like the little child, he will not enter the Kingdom of God.

Matthew 18:2-3

²And Jesus called a little child unto him, and set him in the midst of them, ³And said, Verily I say unto you, Except ye be converted, and become as little children, ye shall not enter into the kingdom of heaven.

Children are simple-minded and have no complications in their minds or reasoning. They literally believe anything you tell them at the foundational stage of their life, that is, ages 0 to 7. Say to a child within this age that you will buy him or her an airplane as a birthday gift, and the child will believe it because of simple-heartedness. The child would not be able to reason to know whether you could afford it, and of what use it is to him or her at that age, because of a simple heart. Children, in the same way, quickly receive and believe the Word of God because they are simple-hearted. The Word of God gives the light that drives away the folly and mischief in children's hearts. The Word of God gives light and understanding that makes one wise. But who will put the Word of God in them? It is the primary responsibility of their parents to do so, not the pastor nor the church.

Deuteronomy 6:5-7

⁵And thou shalt love the LORD thy God with all thine heart, and with all thy soul, and with all thy might. ⁶And these words, which I command thee this day, shall be in thine heart: ⁷And thou shalt teach them diligently unto thy children, and shalt talk of them when thou sittest in thine house, and when thou walkest by the way, and when thou liest down, and when thou risest up.

God commanded parents to diligently teach His Word to their children. The commandment was to the parents and not to the pastors or the Church. The ministers and the church are only there to play a supplementary role in teaching the children the Word of God. Parents are the closest influencers to the children at the foundational stages of their lives. Parents are the most trusted people in a child's life. Children look to their parents for their daily needs and food for nourishment. Therefore, God has rightfully charged parents with this responsibility. Parents must diligently feed their children daily with God's Word for their spiritual nourishment. The earlier the better, so that the children will grow with a sound mind in the fear of God. Able to discern between good and evil, and flee from evil and pursue that which is good in God's sight. Parents who desire to raise godly children must bring their children to the LORD by teaching them God's Word early. Then, God through His Word will teach them the fear of the LORD, and they will depart from evil, do good, live long, and see good in life.

Psalm 34:11-14

11Come, ye children, hearken unto me: I will teach you the fear of the LORD. 12What man is he that desireth life, and loveth many days, that he may see good? 13Keep thy tongue from evil, and thy lips from speaking guile. 14Depart from evil, and do good; seek peace, and pursue it.

When the Bible speaks of training children, it is usually those between the ages of zero and seven. Timothy was taught the Scriptures between the ages of zero to seven (0-7) just like King

Josiah, and Apostle Paul could see it. Paul was only responsible for building on the foundation Timothy's mother, Eunice, and his grandmother Lois had laid. Children will most likely not depart from the ways of God when their parents lay the foundation of their lives with God's Word. Proverbs 22:6, *"Train up a child in the way he should go: and when he is old, he will not depart from it."* It was the entrance of God's Word that gave light, that is, knowledge and understanding, to the child Timothy because he was a child and was naturally simple-hearted.

2 Timothy 3:14-15

14 But continue thou in the things which thou hast learned and hast been assured of, knowing of whom thou hast learned them; 15 And that from a child thou hast known the holy scriptures, which are able to make thee wise unto salvation through faith which is in Christ Jesus.

Imagine a situation where no foundation of God's Word was laid in Timothy's life by his parents, Satan would have seized the occasion to lay an evil foundation in Timothy because there are no vacuums in life. Apostle Paul's efforts would have been like building a structure on a bad foundation, or at best building on a very weak foundation. It would have been very difficult to have the kind of success he had with Pastor Timothy. It was the entrance of God's Word that gave the light of knowledge and understanding to Timothy because he was naturally simple-hearted as a child. With a good foundation of God's Word in a child's life, no matter how far that child goes astray. It will be easier to adjust them back to the foundation of their life by destroying the corrupt structures laid by Satan. And rebuilding godly structures that fit the foundation laid by the parents. The responsibility of feeding the children with a daily supply of God's Word is to both parents. Nonetheless, remember that mothers have the natural disposition to effectively accomplish this task. Children are usually closer and more dependent on their mothers for their daily needs and nourishment at the foundational stage of their lives. Women should learn from the mothers of Prophet Samuel, King Josiah, Pastor Timothy, and other godly women in the Bible who diligently exploited this natural disposition and raised godly children for the LORD. Godly mothers who did a great job of implanting godliness in their sons' lives through God's Word at an early age. The rewards for their labor were fabulous and life-lasting. Diligently emulate their godly examples, and you will get the same outcome in your children's lives.

7.2 Take the Children to Church

The church should be a place where children go to learn about God through His Word and not a Sunday daycare. It should be a place where children are taught to fear and obey God. A place where they are taught about heaven and hell, and how to avoid hell and make heaven. Some parents desire to raise godly children, but do not have time to take their children to church regularly, and some do not take them to church at all. Then some who take their children to church just allow them to run around instead of sitting down to learn God's Word. Those parents tell themselves that they are just children; let them play. That is that goat mentality at work again; let them play, they are just kids (goats). Unfortunately, those children will grow up with the wrong perspective about God's house. They will grow up not taking the house of the LORD or the things of God seriously because that was the foundation laid in them. Therefore, take your children to church and teach them how people ought to behave in the house of the LORD.

Taking your children to church is not just to take them to any place called church but to a Bible-believing and Bible-teaching living church. Some churches in this end-time are just a coven of witches. While some would only serve as a Sunday daycare for your children. Some others are just houses of demonic indoctrination. I am not saying take them to these kinds of churches. If you do, you will only succeed in bewitching and indoctrinating your children with the doctrines of demons. At best, you would have only succeeded in taking them to another daycare that will help you raise big kids (goats); that is, children who do not know the LORD. It is your duty as parents to search out a true Bible-believing and Bible-teaching church that will help you raise godly children for the LORD.

Psalm 122:1

I was glad when they said unto me, Let us go into the house of the LORD.

Why was David glad when people said to him; Let us go to the house of the LORD? David's statement in Psalm 122:1 reveals the foundation his parents laid in his life. His parents laid the godly foundation of taking David to the house of God, and that was why it gave him joy whenever he heard of going to the house of God. Proverbs 22:6, *"Train up a child in the way he should go: and when he is old, he will not depart from it."* It is said that you can't teach an old dog a new trick. Children who are not taken regularly to church by their parents and taught the essence of going to the house of God may not appreciate going to church when they grow up. They most likely will not be glad to go to church because they don't really understand the essence of going to the house of God. The essence of going to the house of God was implanted in David from childhood. David's parents did not just take him to the house of God to play around, but to learn God's Word and to worship Him. David fully understood the essence of going to the house of God. He knew it was to hear the Word of God. David knew that in the house of God, he would find new treasures in God's Word for his prosperity. He was glad to go to the house of God because he was eager to find new treasures in God's Word.

Psalm 119:162

I rejoice at thy word, as one that findeth great spoil.

If you want to raise godly children, take them to a true Bible-believing and Bible-teaching church and teach them the essence of going to church. They are capable of learning. Let God be true and every man a liar. He says to train up a child in the way he should go, and when he grows, he will not depart from it. Do this and you will raise godly children like King David; children after God's heart who will do all His will all the days of their lives.

Psalm 13:22

And when he had removed him, he raised up unto them David to be their king; to whom also he gave testimony, and said, I have found David the son of Jesse, a man after mine own heart, which shall fulfil all my will.

CHAPTER 8

Strive for Parenting and Not Friendship

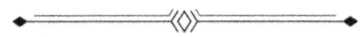

In the contemporary world, parents are taught and encouraged everywhere, even in churches, to strive to be their children's friends. This teaching is erroneous and contrary to the biblical principle of parenting and friendship. You cannot train a godly child by striving to be their friend. Prioritizing friendship over parenting can never produce a godly child. The horse needs a cart for more productivity, but not as much as the cart needs the horse. The cart will be totally unproductive without the horse. On the other hand, the horse can be very productive without the cart but will be much more productive with the cart.

The horse by itself can be very useful and productive. It can carry people around and do a lot of other things. The cart by itself is useless and unproductive, without the horse. It will serve no meaningful purpose without a horse. Parenting is the horse, and friendship is the cart. There is this saying, "Don't put the cart before the horse." When you put the cart before the horse, the cart cannot drag the horse, so they both become unproductive. When you put friendship before parenting, your effort to raise godly children will become futile. Striving for friendship with your children is like putting the cart before the horse; you cannot raise godly children that way. Godly parenting is nurturing and training a child in the fear of the LORD. You can still raise godly children without trying to be their friends. Once you succeed with parenting, friendship ensues automatically. John 15:14, *"Ye are my friends, if ye do whatsoever I command you."* Remember that the horse is still very productive without the cart; you can raise godly children by simply focusing on godly parenting.

8.1 Biblical Principle of Parenting and Friendship

The biblical principle of parenting and friendship is parenting before friendship; obedience to parents' instructions before friendship. Once obedience through parenting is achieved, friendship with the children is automatic, even without laboring for it. According to Jesus, children should earn their parents' friendship through obedience to their parents' instructions.

John 15:14-15

14YE ARE MY FRIENDS, IF YE DO WHATSOEVER I COMMAND YOU. 15Henceforth I call you not servants; for the servant knoweth not what his lord doeth: but I have called you friends; for all things that I have heard of my Father I have made known unto you.

Now look at Jesus' condition for His children to become His friend: if ye do whatsoever I command you. That is how children should become their parents' friends too. When they do whatsoever their parents command them. The children should be the ones to labor to become their parents' friends through obedience. Throughout the Scripture, Jesus often dealt with and taught believers as a father would. Jesus, the LORD and creator of mankind, is the heavenly Father of Christians. Parents teach and train their children to know, understand, and obey their instructions. Jesus, being a Father to Christians, said in John

163

15:14 that His children can only become His friends if they obey His commandments. Jesus is saying that His primary focus as a Father is for His children to obey His instructions, and only then will they become His friends. Jesus is saying that He does not strive for friendship with His children but for parenting and that His friendship is the benefit of an obedient child. God does not call all His children friends but only those who honor Him through obedience to His commandments. In God's dealings with Israel as His children, He only called Abraham His friend. God called him His friend because of his unfeigned obedience, and the rest of Israel He called His servants.

Isaiah 41:8

But thou, Israel, art my servant, Jacob whom I have chosen, the seed of Abraham my friend.

James 2:21-23

[21]Was not Abraham our father justified by works, when he had offered Isaac his son upon the altar? [22]Seest thou how faith wrought with his works, and by works was faith made perfect? [23]And the scripture was fulfilled which saith, Abraham believed God, and it was imputed unto him for righteousness: and he was called the Friend of God.

It was Abraham's works that validated his faith and earned him the friendship status with God. This is to say, it was his obedience to God's commandments that authenticated his belief in God and earned him the friendship status with God. Therefore, we can say that Abraham became God's friend because he obeyed God's commandments. Abraham, God's child, obeyed the commandments of God, his heavenly Father, and became a friend to his Father. John 15:14, ***"Ye are my***

friends, if ye do whatsoever I command you." This is the biblical principle of parenting and friendship from the Old Testament to the New Testament. It has not changed and will not change. Parents who desire to raise godly children for the LORD must follow this biblical order: parenting before friendship. Parents should never strive to be their children's friends but should rather strive for godly parenting. The children are the ones to labor to become their parents' friends through obedience.

The Scripture unequivocally states the principle of parenting and friendship in John 15:14, **"Ye are my friends, if ye do whatsoever I command you."** In other words, children earn their parents' friendship through absolute obedience to their parents' godly commandments. God was confident in His friend and son Abraham that he would command his children to keep the way of the LORD.

Genesis 18:19

For I know him (Abraham), that he will command his children and his household after him, and they shall keep the way of the LORD, to do justice and judgment; that the LORD may bring upon Abraham that which he hath spoken of him.

This is a perfect example of godly parenting. It shows that Abraham did not strive to be his children's friend but rather strove for godly parenting. This is evident in the life of Isaac, his son. Abraham succeeded in raising a godly child for the LORD. One would have thought that Abraham and Sarah would have pampered and strove to be best friends with Isaac. Considering that Isaac was their only child and the only seed of promise to

Abraham. However, many Christian parents strive for their children's friendship, without being in Abraham and Sarah's condition. How much more would they do so when they have only one child? Abraham and Sarah did not fool around, striving to be Isaac's best friend, but they stood their ground on parenting Isaac. They commanded him to keep the way of the LORD. Isaac never departed from the godly training and commandments of his parents. Proverbs 22:6, *"Train up a child in the way he should go: and when he is old, he will not depart from it."* Hence, God also kept His promise to Abraham, to bless all the nations of the earth through his seed. Genesis 22:18, *"And in thy seed shall all the nations of the earth be blessed; because thou hast obeyed my voice."* God kept his promise because Abraham obeyed His voice. It was not only for obeying His command to sacrifice Isaac, but his total obedience to all of God's commandments, which included commanding his children to keep God's way. Why did God speak confidently about Abraham that he will command his children to keep His way? It is because God has proven Abraham to be an obedient child, and for this reason, God called him His friend. Christian parents, are you also an obedient child to God? Could God also speak confidently about you that you will command your children to keep the way of the LORD? Or you are just a disobedient child who will not obey the commandments of God, your heavenly Father. I pray that the latter is not the case.

8.2 The Place of Friendship in Parenting.

Please do not become King Nebuchadnezzar to your children. We are not trying to establish a King Nebuchadnezzar and his subjects type relationship, but a parent-child relationship. Parents must establish sound godly discipline that will ensure their children have a healthy fear and respect for them enough to obey their instructions. All this is not to say that parents should not purposefully extend the hand of friendship to their children. Rather, doing that should be a reward for their obedience and not an incentive to get their obedience. This is not to say that parents should do away with friendship in their parenting. This is simply saying that it must occupy a secondary place in parenting. The place of friendship in parenting is secondary. Who you are to your children is a parent. Therefore, play your role as a parent. When you add friendship to your parenting, ensure it takes a secondary place, and you will be more productive in your parenting. Parenting becomes much more productive as the horse will become much more productive with a cart attached to it than it would have been without a cart. After you have achieved obedience in your children through godly parenting and a friendly relationship is borne, ensure the friendly relationship stays secondary, always remember that your primary duty to your children is parenting.

God, the heavenly Father, as a parent, did not put friendship ahead of parenting. Nevertheless, His relationship with His children is not the Nebuchadnezzar terror-type relationship, but a loving Father and children relationship. Despite God's loving relationship with His children, He still maintained a parenting first principle with His children. He disciplined His children promptly and kept friendship with His children in a secondary place as a reward for obedience. John 15:14, ***"Ye are my friends, if ye do whatsoever I command you."***

Hebrews 12:6-7

⁶For whom the Lord loveth he chasteneth, and scourgeth every son whom he receiveth. ⁷If ye endure chastening, God dealeth with you as with sons; for what son is he whom the father chasteneth not?

Abraham believed and obeyed God and became God's friend forever. God also promised to bless all the nations of the earth through Abraham's seed as a reward for his obedience. Genesis 22:18, *"And in thy seed shall all the nations of the earth be blessed; because thou hast obeyed my voice."* This blessing was conditional on Abraham being able to raise a godly child on whom God could depend. Abraham applied the same godly principle of parenting first in raising his son, Isaac, and succeeded in raising a godly child that God could depend on for the blessings of all the nations of the earth.

Genesis 18:19

For I know him (Abraham), that he will command his children and his household after him, and they shall keep the way of the LORD, to do justice and judgment; that the LORD may bring upon Abraham that which he hath spoken of him.

Parents who want to raise godly children must follow the same principle of our heavenly Father. Parents should not strive for friendship over parenting. Know that you are a parent, and stand your ground on parenting. Do not be afraid that your children will be angry with you. When your children have learned to obey your instructions, then friendship can ensue. Do not put the cart before the horse; you will make the horse completely unproductive. Parenting is the horse, and friendship is the cart;

do not put friendship before parenting; you will make godly parenting completely unproductive. Hence, your efforts to raise godly children for the LORD would become futile.

CHAPTER 9

Protect Your Children from Destruction

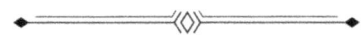

Protecting children from anything capable of destroying or harming them physically, mentally, and spiritually is one of the principal duties of parents. Children are very vulnerable to all kinds of destructive agents and harmful influences. Their susceptibility to negative influence and destruction is due to their ignorance and simple-mindedness. These destructive agents and influences could come from ungodly knowledge, other children, and adults. Parents have the responsibility of protecting their children from all destructive agents and harmful influences until they become of age and able to protect themselves. Unfortunately, this is not the case with most parents in the contemporary world. Parents have armed their children with knowledge that is greater than them and left them to protect themselves. What they have done could be likened to buying assault weapons like AK47 and AR15 and handing them over to their children of four and six years old, to protect themselves. Parents do this in contemporary times because of ignorance and for the freedom of pleasure time, and to work as many hours as possible. These parents then feel good about themselves because they have armed their children with enough knowledge for them to protect themselves. It is not wise to arm children to protect themselves; parents are to arm themselves as adults and protect their children.

Psalms 82:3-6

³Defend the poor and fatherless: do justice to the afflicted and needy. ⁴Deliver the poor and needy: rid them out of the hand of the wicked. ⁵They know not, neither will they understand; they walk on in darkness: all the foundations of the earth are out of course. ⁶I have said, Ye are gods; and all of you are children of the Most High.

God is saying that we should defend the poor and the fatherless. In other words, we should defend the weak and vulnerable in our midst. Why must we defend the weak and vulnerable in our midst? We must defend them because they are not capable of defending themselves. Who is weaker and more vulnerable than children? Children are ignorant, lack understanding, and cannot protect themselves. Psalms 82:5. *"They know not, neither will they understand; they walk on in darkness: all the foundations of the earth are out of course."* The whole world is out of course, from the foundation and heading to utter destruction because parents have abandoned weak and vulnerable children to protect themselves instead of protecting them. Children are the foundation and posterity of humanity. If they are left to destruction in their weak and vulnerable state, when they lack the understanding needed to protect themselves. Then where is the hope for humanity? God is saying that all are His children, including the vulnerable children who must be protected. Psalm 82:6, **"I have said, Ye are gods; and all of you are children of the Most High."**

171

9.1 Destruction by Lack of Knowledge

Children are very vulnerable to harm and destruction because they are weak in strength and mind. Most families live in physically safe environments, and people would naturally move to physically safe places to raise a family. They live in physically safe and secure houses to protect their families from physical harm. Some parents have also forearmed themselves with firearms to protect themselves and their families from harm and destruction. Parents also tend to keep a watchful eye over their children both at home and outside of the home to ensure that they are not physically harmed. Therefore, for the most part, parents usually protect their children from physical harm and destruction. Most parents can see their children's frailty in stature and strength. Nonetheless, can they see and understand the frailty of their children's minds? Many parents in contemporary times have failed to really understand the frailty of their children's minds. While it is very important to protect children from physical harm. Nonetheless, it's of utmost importance to protect their minds from the harm and destruction of the lack of knowledge. Knowledge is a very powerful defensive and offensive asset. It is a must-have asset for defense, offense, and prosperity. The lack of relevant and necessary knowledge required for a person's development, safety, and prosperity could be deadly.

Hosea 4:6

My people are destroyed for lack of knowledge: because thou hast rejected knowledge, I will also reject thee, that thou shalt be no priest to me: seeing thou hast forgotten the law of thy God, I will also forget thy children.

Parents must provide adequate godly and circular knowledge relevant to their children's development, safety, and prosperity. However, many parents in contemporary times have failed to provide adequate knowledge of God's Word necessary for their children's safety and prosperity. As a result of this, many children are being destroyed. That is why many youths are incarcerated for crimes, and many die from drugs, gang violence, and gun violence across the United States. Others are destroyed by STDs and abortions of unwanted pregnancies resulting from their promiscuous lifestyles. A promiscuous lifestyle they learned from schools, Hollywood, and the entertainment and fashion industries. This is also the same across the world, as inflicted by the various evils that have taken over the youths of that society or nation. This is just to speak of earthly destruction that can be observed. How much more of the eternal destruction that has engulfed these youths and adults who have perished without the adequate knowledge of God's Word that could have saved them from eternal destruction. It is a pity!

Psalm 9:17

The wicked shall be turned into hell, and all the nations that forget God.

Isaiah 66:24

And they shall go forth, and look upon the carcases of the men that have transgressed against me: for their worm shall not die, neither shall their fire be quenched; and they shall be an abhorring unto all flesh.

Hosea 4:6

My people are destroyed for lack of knowledge: because thou hast rejected knowledge, I will also reject thee, that thou shalt be no priest to me: seeing thou hast forgotten the law of thy God, I will also forget thy children.

I pray for you as a parent or would-be parent who is reading this, that your eyes of understanding be enlightened to see and understand that the most important knowledge for your children's safety and prosperity is the Word of God. That you may understand that your children's protection, safety, and prosperity in this life and the life to come rest in their adequate knowledge of God's Word, and their obedience to the same. It is the knowledge of God's Word in your children that will put the fear of God in their hearts and cause them to do right. The Word of God will keep them away from evil. It will produce the godly characters that will keep them safe from destruction and death, and prosper them in this life and the life to come. Therefore, parents, protect your children with adequate knowledge of God's Word.

Psalm 119:9-11

9Wherewithal shall a young man cleanse his way? by taking heed thereto according to thy word. 10With my whole heart have I sought thee: O let me not wander from thy commandments. 11Thy word have I hid in mine heart, that I might not sin against thee.

Psalm 119:116-117

116Uphold me according unto thy word, that I may live: and let me not be ashamed of my hope. 117Hold thou me up, and I shall be safe: and I will have respect unto thy statutes continually.

I say adequate knowledge because most people have some knowledge of God's Word and teach their children the same.

Insufficient knowledge of the Word of God is not enough to adequately protect them from destruction and death in this life and life to come. Parents must look for a true church of God where the whole truth of God's Word is taught for holy living. I strongly recommend and encourage anyone who wants to protect their family from destruction and death to connect with Holiness Revival Movement Worldwide (HOREMOW). It is a ministry where the whole Word of God is taught in perfect doctrinal truth for holy living. You can follow the Movement and its teachings on YouTube and Facebook and join the location nearest to you.

9.2: Destruction by Ungodly and Unnecessary Knowledge

Infusing ungodly and unnecessary knowledge that is irrelevant to a person's development, safety, and prosperity could be harmful and deadly. This applies to both adults and children, but for this book, we will focus on the children. Parents who want to raise godly children for the LORD must understand how deadly ungodly and unnecessary knowledge is, and protect their children from such. You would never have craved for ice cream unless you knew there was such a thing as ice cream and that it is very sweet to the taste and delightful to consume. This was the predicament that Eve found herself in, which destroyed her and Adam, and consequently, the human race. Eve was peaceful in the Garden of Eden for many years untold without any desire for the Tree of the Knowledge of Good and Evil until Satan deceived her about the Tree. That unnecessary knowledge aroused her desire to eat the fruit of the Tree. If Satan had not armed Eve with such false and unnecessary knowledge, she would never have desired to eat of the Tree. But as soon as that deceitful knowledge came from Satan, the desire for it was born. Eve, being a babe in knowledge and experience, could not exercise knowledge, willpower, and maturity to resist being destroyed by that ungodly and unnecessary knowledge from Satan.

Genesis 3:1-6

¹Now the serpent was more subtle than any beast of the field which the LORD God had made. And he said unto the woman, Yea, hath God said, Ye shall not eat of every tree of the garden? ²And the woman said unto the serpent, we may eat of the fruit of the trees of the garden: ³But of the fruit of the tree which is in the midst of the garden, God hath said, Ye shall not eat of it, neither shall ye touch it, lest ye die. ⁴And the serpent said unto the woman, Ye shall not surely die: ⁵For God doth know that in the day ye eat thereof, then your eyes shall be opened, and ye shall be as gods, knowing good and evil. ⁶And when the woman saw that the tree was good for food, and that it was pleasant to the eyes, and a tree to be desired to make one wise, she took of the fruit thereof, and did eat, and gave also unto her husband with her; and he did eat.

While adults may be able to exercise their willpower, knowledge, and maturity to resist destruction from ungodly and unnecessary knowledge, children are very susceptible to becoming victims. Ungodly and unnecessary knowledge is very destructive to children because;

1. They have not yet built the moral framework that will help them understand evil and know when and how to depart from it.

2. Their brain is not fully developed to reason and fully understand the potential harm of their choices and actions in the short and long run.

3. Whatever knowledge they are often exposed to forms the building blocks of their developing brain, and harder to reverse the effects.

These three factors make the children's minds very vulnerable, and Satan knows this, especially that of the third. Proverbs 22:6 ***"Train up a child in the way he should go: and when he is old, he will not depart from it."*** Taking advantage of this, Satan has strategically introduced many ungodly and unnecessary harmful and deadly knowledge to the children through his various kiddifying agents. However, for this chapter, I will focus on the school system. I cannot exhaust all the ungodly and unnecessary destructive knowledge being infused into the children through the school system, but to mention a few: the Big Bang Theory, Macroevolution Theory, and Child Sex Education.

The Big Bang and Macroevolution Theories:

The Big Bang Theory and Macroevolution Theory indoctrinate children to believe that humans and all life came into existence through a long evolutionary journey that started from a Big Bang (explosion) billions of years ago. I used the word "indoctrinate" because that is the real aim of these theories. These theories are doctrines of an alternate religious belief meant to indoctrinate children to do away with God, and that religion is Atheism. While these theories are disguised as science studies, in actuality, there is nothing scientific about them. They miserably fail the simple scientific method litmus test of empiricism; they cannot be observed nor repeated. The scientific method is a repeatable process of data collection to hypothesize (make assumptions) for empirical (observable) experimentation. The Big Bang Theory claims that an atomic explosion about 13.8 billion years ago formed the universe, which includes the Earth. Then, Macroevolution Theory claims that all living things evolved from nonliving things (rock) that formed from the Big Bang after billions of years. The summation of their doctrine is that all existence evolved from this atomic explosion – The Big Bang. This explosion formed the universe, and the rocks evolved into amoeba to sponges to crayfish to fish to reptiles to rodents to pigs to apes to humans, and could no longer evolve into new species. Someone should please make this make sense, apart from a mythical religious indoctrination.

These Big Bang and Macroevolution Atheistic doctrines taught to children in schools cannot be observed nor repeated. They are mythology at its best and are theories as they are rightfully called. A theory is a belief, philosophy, opinion, a notion. The Big Bang and Macroevolution theories require even greater faith to believe in than one would need to believe in God. This is so because these stories are estranged from reality; they are myths, and have no empirical point of reference to reality. The empirical data on atomic explosions known to man (Hiroshima & Nagasaki) are contrary to the Big Bang's claims. The atomic bombs the United States dropped on Hiroshima and Nagasaki in 1945 did not and have not evolved into life forms. They only brought massive destruction to lives and properties. No one has observed the repeat of the process of Macroevolution, that is, the evolution of one species into another. We have not seen an ape in the process of turning into a human, yet they claim Macroevolution is an ongoing process.

The truth is that the stories of the Big Bang and Macroevolution are mythological doctrines of the religion of Atheism. The sole purpose of the Big Bang and Macroevolution Theories is to eliminate creationism and faith in God. Then create a dominant religion of atheism disguised as an academic scientific study. Satan's goal with this move is to fill the world with immoral intellectual fools (Atheists).

Psalms 14:1

The fool hath said in his heart, there is no God. They are corrupt, they have done abominable works, there is none that doeth good.

Psalm 53:1

The fool hath said in his heart, there is no God. Corrupt are they, and have done abominable iniquity: there is none that doeth good.

Romans 1:20-22

[20]For the invisible things of him from the creation of the world are clearly seen, being understood by the things that are made, even his eternal power and Godhead; so that they are without excuse: [21]Because that, when they knew God, they glorified him not as God, neither were thankful; but became vain in their imaginations, and their foolish heart was darkened. [22]Professing themselves to be wise, they became fools,

Satan has captured the school system as one of his worship centers and agents for indoctrination into his religion of Atheism. Through the schools, he indoctrinates the young minds of the children to raise immoral intellectual fools (Atheists) for

Christian parents. That is to say, children who do not know the LORD nor care about the things of the LORD. Simply put, children who hate God. All these are Satan's efforts to lay the foundation of your children's lives and condition their minds to conform to his evil world thought process. This strange religion of Atheism then forms the foundation of their lives, and they most likely will not depart from it. The school has become a great tool in the hands of Satan in the world to accomplish his task of raising children who are alienated from God. This is the main reason Christian parents often see a 180-degree turnaround in their children's character and attitude towards God once they start school. If you abandon the most valuable period of training your children in the hands of Satan through schools. Satan will succeed in raising immoral intellectual fools (Atheists) for you. Children who do not know the LORD nor care about the things of the LORD. Children who hate the LORD.

Christian parents who want to raise godly children for the LORD must not abandon their children in the hands of the school system. They must labor hard to lay a solid knowledge of God's Word in them before they start school and while in school. They must create time to daily check with their children on what they were taught in school and lovingly redirect their thoughts to affirm the truth of God's Word on any lesson contrary to truth. 2Corinthians 10:5, *Casting down imaginations, and every high thing that exalteth itself against the knowledge of God, and bringing into captivity every thought to the obedience of Christ;*

Romans 12:2

And be not conformed to this world: but be ye transformed by the renewing of your mind, that ye may prove what is that good, and acceptable, and perfect will of God.

The Bible admonishes that we should not be conformed to this world. That is, do not follow the world's school of thought. Do not think like those who do not know God and do not behave like them. Parents are responsible for ensuring that their children do not conform to Satan's evil world's atheistic thought process. Parents must labor hard to lay a solid foundation of biblical truth in their children's lives before they get into college/university. Your children should have a sound biblical worldview before getting into higher institutions of learning. They should be able to view everything in life through God's Word. At that point, the Word of God should be their Ultimate Source of Authority (USA) for the validation of truth on any subject matter. Achieving this requires great sacrificial commitment from parents. Failure to achieve this before the children get into college/university is a catalyst for raising immoral intellectual fools (Atheist).

During my first degree at Salem State University, I had to challenge three of my professors to defend God's Word and Christianity. The school system these days is primarily focused on erasing anything God from the minds of the students. On one of these occasions, I was in a history class. Our history professor was verbose and a proud man, and as he taught that day, it was a full-scale attack on religion, especially Christianity. He so much demonized Christianity and intellectually debased it. It was so bad that any Christian student in the class would be so intimidated to be identified as one. If you were already known as one, you would feel like hiding under the desk if possible and waiting for everyone to leave before sneaking out to go home in shame. At some point, I was also intimidated because of the great authority this proud and verbose professor wielded in class. Then I thought to myself that there was no need to say anything, I knew the truth, and there was nothing he could say or do to change my biblical worldview. Then, as if the Holy Spirit said to me; Look around. I looked around and could see the multitude of young minds that filled the class with their eyes glued on him as they listened in amazement. Then I knew I had to speak up for their sake. I raised my hand as the professor continued to speak, and after a while, he stopped and allowed me to speak. I stood up and asked him an experiential question based on what he was teaching, and he answered, "I don't know." I asked him a second question, and he also said he didn't know the answer. Then I asked the third question, and this time he was a little embarrassed and shrugged his shoulders and said I really don't know. And I said to him; Then you should not destroy what you don't know. Then I gave an explanatory answer to my first question and said that I would stop at that because I didn't want to use up his class time. And as I wanted to sit down, almost all the students exclaimed at the same time that he should allow me. They wanted to hear what I had to say about the other two questions. I looked at him and he beckoned to me to continue. After my explanatory answers to the other two questions, the atmosphere in the class changed. The students were perplexed as their eyes of understanding were enlightened to see God from an experiential perspective. The once proud, verbose professor became gentle and spoke with meekness. When the class was over, and I was about to head to the door, the professor called me, and when I came, he asked, "Who are you?" I told him that I was a Christian and his student, but he was not satisfied with my answer. And asked, I mean, "Who are you? What is your profession?"

I also challenge my English professor in class and my biology professor in writing to defend God's Word and my Christian worldview. In both cases, God was also mightily glorified. The English professor was teaching us poetry that day and used some verses from the Book of Psalms. In his teaching, he referred to the Book of Psalms as just a poetry book without divine inspiration. This is one of the subtle ways that Satan uses these professors, knowingly or unknowingly, to destroy and remove the knowledge of God from Christian students in schools. Students highly esteem their professors as intellectuals and highly knowledgeable. Therefore, many Christian students in that class that day, without adequate knowledge of God's Word and personal walk experience with God, may start disbelieving the Bible as the Word of God. They are likely to leave the class thinking they have been deceived all along to believe that the Bible is inspired by God, by their parents and pastors. The thought of this clouded my mind as the professor taught the class. I then raised my hand and he beckoned to me to speak. I spoke and asked him questions as the Holy Spirit inspired me. I spoke and asked questions from an experiential perspective because of my biblical knowledge and walk with God. The professor could not answer my questions, and I said to him that he should not destroy what he does not know. After class, he called me for a conversation. In our discussion, I expounded on the validity and efficacy of God's Word based on personal empirical evidence. He confessed to me that he used to believe in the Bible's divine inspiration and that it was life events that had led him otherwise. Through our discussion, he regained faith in the Word of God. He then promised that he would start taking his two daughters to church so they could grow up with the knowledge of God. The professor and I became friends since that day, and he would contact me whenever he had spiritual or biblical questions. He called me to preach at his brother's funeral, and he has attended at least three of my special church programs. We still speak regularly and visit each other.

The case of my biology professor was when he gave us an assignment to write an essay on evolution based on an article he gave us to read. The professor prewarned us not to write that evolution is nonsense, and we should remember that he is the one doing the marking. In my paper, I first articulated my knowledge of evolution and the article he gave us to read. Then I proceeded to articulate my knowledge of biblical facts on the creation of the earth and life. I focused on biblical facts that can be empirically verified. I quoted and wrote Bible verses on my paper for references. I then made my arguments and stated at least once that macroevolution is preposterous. I concluded my paper with one or two questions for him to answer on evolution, if he thinks otherwise.

Then I was working overnight and used to do my assignments at work. I gave my paper to two of my Christian coworkers, one was a pastor. After reading, they said I should not submit that paper because my professor will give me zero. They counseled that I should separate church work from school work. I told them that I would be very happy and fulfilled to get zero as long as he gets to read my paper. I told them I believed what I had written would pursue him for the rest of his life, irrespective of how he views it. I went ahead and submitted my paper without making any changes based on their counsel. The next class, when I got my paper from my biology professor. He gave me 93% and remarked on my paper, "Cliff, this is a very thoughtful essay. I have never thought of it in this light." After class, he asked if I could find time any day to meet for a discussion that he would like to know more.

I survived all the direct and indirect attacks on my faith in God at the university because I had a solid godly foundation. I escaped with my Christian worldview because of the marvelous work God did in my life through the sound godly foundation my parents laid in my life. Parents are responsible for ensuring that their children do not conform to Satan's evil world's atheistic thought process. This must be accomplished at the foundational level of the children's lives, from ages zero to seven. Parents must sacrifice time and resources to lay a sound biblical foundation in their children's lives. I cannot overemphasize the importance of parents' role in ensuring that their children do not become immoral intellectual fools (Atheists) through the school system. Parents should always remember that their children are their only assets with eternal value. There is no amount of sacrifice and investment too great to protect and preserve such assets. God had confidence in Abraham that he would do all it takes, and give all it would cost to raise Him godly children. Could God say the same of you?

Genesis 18:19

For I know him, that he will command his children and his household after him, and they shall keep the way of the

LORD, to do justice and judgment; that the LORD may bring upon Abraham that which he hath spoken of him.

Child Sex Education:

Child sex education is the greatest scam of the century by Satan on parents. Satan, in his wisdom and subtilty, introduced child sex education in schools. This he did in the pretense of arming the children with sexual knowledge to protect themselves from sexual abuse. However, his actual aim is to corrupt their innocent minds and indoctrinate them into all manner of sexual immorality and deviance to defile their purity. Many parents were deceived into believing that it was a great idea and accepted child sex education for their minor children. Why did parents easily fall for this child sex education scam? Because the problem of children getting sexually abused is very real. Children are often sexually abused by adults more than ever before. Parents are living daily with the fear of their children being sexually abused, and because of this, they accepted Satan's proposal. The question is, how did this problem of sexual abuse of children become a pandemic in contemporary times? It was Satan who created this child sexual abuse pandemic. This he did by sexualizing everything; pumping the world with pornography, sexualizing the movie and music industry with sexual lyrics, nudity, and all kinds of sexual acts. Sexualizing women and men to dress half-naked and become sexual figures on the streets and in society. Even the little children are sexualized in the way they dress, just like the adults. The society is sexually charged at all times through adverts, music, movies, pornography, and in real life. Hence, the world is filled with adults and children who are sexually charged, who do not know God nor fear him, and without self-control. Some, having no place to discharge their tense sexual desires, take advantage of vulnerable innocent children. Now with this problem he created, which made parents apprehensive about their children, he then proffers a solution to protect their children. The solution of arming their innocent children with sexual education to help them know when a predator is advancing sexually, so they can protect themselves. Sounds good, right? Then to what benefit is it to Satan to proffer a solution to protect your children, whom he earnestly seeks to destroy? Maybe you are not aware that child sex education proceeded from Satan? I hope you can now see the signature of Satan in it, "Order out of Chaos". Satan's hallmark of creating a problem that will cause apprehension and proffering a misleading solution that will further advance his agenda.

It is the parents' responsibility to arm themselves with knowledge and create time to guard and protect their children from sexual abuse. Instead, most parents have armed their children with sexual knowledge far greater than they could handle and left them to protect themselves. These parents then feel good about themselves because they have armed their children with enough knowledge to protect themselves. Arming your children with sexual knowledge far greater than they could handle is like buying them assault weapons like AK47s and AR15s to protect themselves from intruders. The children will surely play the game of police and thief as soon as you are gone and will kill themselves with the assault weapons before any intruder who may or may not come. It is not wise to arm children to protect themselves; parents are to arm themselves as adults and protect their children. Now, let us approach this subject matter empirically, what we have observed and experienced. As a young child growing up, what did you do with all the knowledge you acquired from TV, from your parents, or school? You were so eager to exercise that knowledge, you found out ways to practice it. After watching wrestling, you wrestled with your siblings. After watching detective movies, you played the game of police and thief with your siblings and friends. After watching music artists perform, you devised a mic, be it a stick or anything else, and started singing and performing like that artist. After observing your mother cook food, you mimicked the same in your play. Everything you learned and observed as a child, you were eager to find ways to exercise that knowledge. Children are always curious to practice what they have learned. They are always eager to find out what will happen if they try something, even the very same thing you said they should not do.

This was the case for Eve, she was peaceful in the Garden for many years untold without any desire for the Tree of Good and Evil until Satan deceitfully educated her about the Tree of Good and Evil. That false and unnecessary knowledge aroused the curiosity in Eve to want to eat the fruit of the Tree. If Satan had not armed Eve with such false and unnecessary knowledge, she would never have desired to eat of the tree. But as soon as that deceitful knowledge came from Satan, the desire for the fruit of the Tree was born. She became restless and eager to find out what would happen if she ate the fruit of the Tree.

Genesis 3:4-6

⁴And the serpent said unto the woman, Ye shall not surely die: ⁵For God doth know that in the day ye eat thereof, then your eyes shall be opened, and ye shall be as gods, knowing good and evil. ⁶And when the woman saw that the tree was good for food, and that it was pleasant to the eyes, and a tree to be desired to make one wise, she took of the fruit thereof, and did eat, and gave also unto her husband with her; and he did eat.

If Eve had not acquired such false and damning knowledge about the Tree from Satan, she would never have desired to eat the fruit of the Tree. My mother told me that their parents told them in their days that they should not allow any man to touch them because they would become pregnant. Therefore, they fled from anything that appeared to look like a man. This was all the Parental Guide (PG) knowledge they needed as children to keep themselves safe. They never got corrupted, and most of them were virgins when they married. All that Eve and Adam needed to keep them safe from the Tree of Good and Evil was the PG knowledge they received from their Father, the Almighty God.

Genesis 2:16-17

[16]And the LORD God commanded the man, saying, of every tree of the garden thou mayest freely eat: [17]But of the tree of the knowledge of good and evil, thou shalt not eat of it: for in the day that thou eatest thereof thou shalt surely die.

The deceitful knowledge Eve received from Satan about the Tree of the Knowledge of Good and Evil aroused her desire and curiosity to eat the forbidden fruit. In the same way will the knowledge of sex education will arouse the curiosity in your children and cause them to corrupt themselves by eating the forbidden fruit. Then, the corrupted children will ensure to corrupt other children just as Eve ensured to corrupt Adam. Your children will look for every opportunity to experiment and practice all the explicit child sex education they were taught in school. If Satan had not armed your children with such ungodly and unnecessary sexual knowledge, they would never have desired to eat the forbidden fruit. But as soon as Satan introduced sexual knowledge to them, the desire for sex was born. You have armed them with knowledge greater than they could handle. You have given them assault weapons, they will surely play the game of police and thief and kill themselves with it. They will surely experiment and practice with their siblings, relatives, and friends, all the sexual knowledge you have loaded them with. Oh! They can't wait to practice them; they are restless and eager to know what will happen when they do them. This is why incest now occurs at an alarming rate. Since the children do not have much opportunity to practice their sexual knowledge outside, their siblings and cousins provide ample opportunity for practice. They become curious to know more and to watch real sexual acts. Satan, being very clever, has earlier made the internet available to them and has handed them all kinds of electronic devices through their parents. And through their electronic devices, they are able to access the pornography that Satan has already flooded the internet with in readiness for them. As HOREMOW North America Youth and Children Overseer. I have had to deal with several cases of children as young as nine years, both male and female, who are addicted to pornography. These children will not sleep at night because they are busy all night watching pornography. Their minds were made restless because of the sexual education they were taught in school at a very tender age.

The children completely lose their innocence and purity through the sexual knowledge they are loaded with through child sex education. They are corrupted by it, and they corrupt themselves and others. They become the children of Satan. They become defiled and cannot be raptured if Jesus Christ were to come to rapture the Church. They become disqualified to enter heaven, peradventure, when a tragedy occurs and they die young because they have lost their innocence and purity. Through this child sex education, Satan also sexually indoctrinates children into all kinds of immoral sexual deviance, LGBTQ+. They label them as alternative lifestyles. Why is Satan doing this? Because he knows the Scripture. Proverbs 22:6 ***"Train up a child in the way he should go: and when he is old, he will not depart from it."*** With the combination of other evil knowledge like Macroevolution and Big Bang theories, the children are being loaded with in schools. These children will grow into sexually immoral intellectual fools (Atheists). They most likely will not depart from it except there is a divine intervention. This is how Satan fuels and sustains his LGBTQ+ community and all the sexual perversion in the world. He catches them young by polluting and distorting their reasoning at a very tender age through the school system. Save your children from Satan and eternal damnation in hellfire. Resist child sex education for your children with every breath in you. May the LORD grant you the wisdom and grace needed to save your children from the grip of Satan, in Jesus' name, Amen.

9.3 Protect Your Children from Mine

Protect your children from mine! But you are my pastor! Yes, but please, protect your children from mine, and I will likewise do the same. Just because a child is your pastor's child does not make them a good child. Children are not godly simply because they are from a godly home and have godly parents. Any child you allow to be your children's friend should qualify on their own merit. By their fruits, you shall know the godly and the ungodly ones. That is, by their character, you shall know the corrupt children and keep your children away from such, irrespective of whose child they are. The Bible is clear on this, that you can identify the godly and ungodly children by their character.

Proverbs 20:11

Even a child is known by his doings, whether his work be pure, and whether it be right.

Matthew 7: 16-18

[16]Ye shall know them by their fruits. Do men gather grapes of thorns, or figs of thistles? [17]Even so every good tree bringeth forth good fruit; but a corrupt tree bringeth forth evil fruit. [18]A good tree cannot bring forth evil fruit, neither can a corrupt tree bring forth good fruit.

You must fight hard to protect your children from corrupt children if you want to raise godly children for the LORD. The greatest sources of negative influence on children are their peers. This is why you often hear of peer pressure. My parents did an excellent job of protecting us from other children. I would give them an A+ grade. When I was growing up as a child, we were five boys and one girl. I was the second born, and our sister was the last born at that time. My mother had the baby of the family many years later. At the time, I was living with someone in a different state because of school. Growing up, our father would not even allow us to play with the neighbors next door, not to talk of those of the next house. We would be in serious trouble if he came back and heard or caught anyone playing with the neighbor. Our father was a practicing Christian and a very godly man. He held pastors and spiritual leaders in high honor but never allowed us to mingle with their children. We only mingled with our cousins once a year during Christmas. All our mingling with other children ended at school. He never permitted us as children to have friends, visit, or be visited by any child, although we were boys and only the last child at that time was a girl. In all honesty, what knowledge and discernment do children have that will enable them to choose friends? What criteria will a child use to set his or her standard for friendship? As an adult, how many of your childhood friends from primary school, even up to High school, are you still in contact with? The childhood period is not a time for picking friends. Rather, it is the time to train and lay the foundation of a child's life. My parents did a perfect job in their time by protecting us from other children. How much more do parents need to protect their children from other children in this evil day and age? That the internet and woke ideologies have corrupted almost all children? Eli was the high priest in Israel whom all Israel looked up to for the Word of God and justice, and yet his children were the sons of Belial (Satan).

1Samuel 2:12,22

¹²Now the sons of Eli were sons of Belial; they knew not the LORD. ²²Now Eli was very old, and heard all that his sons did unto all Israel; and how they lay with the women that assembled at the door of the tabernacle of the congregation.

The huge mistake many Christian parents make is accepting other children into their homes and children's lives based on their parents' records or their relationship with their parents. His parents are God-fearing, he is my best friend's child, he is my pastor's child, he is my brother/sister's child, etcetera. These are not criteria for permitting a child into your children's lives.

Parents could be as God-fearing as Prophet Samuel and walk uprightly before God, and yet their children are corrupt.

1Samuel 12:3-5

³Behold, here I am: witness against me before the LORD, and before his anointed: whose ox have I taken? or whose ass have I taken? or whom have I defrauded? whom have I oppressed? or of whose hand have I received any bribe to blind mine eyes therewith? and I will restore it you. ⁴And they said, Thou hast not defrauded us, nor oppressed us, neither hast thou taken ought of any man's hand. ⁵And he said unto them, The LORD is witness against you, and his anointed is witness this day, that ye have not found ought in my hand. And they answered, He is witness.

1Samuel 8:1-3

¹And it came to pass, when Samuel was old, that he made his sons judges over Israel. ²Now the name of his firstborn was Joel; and the name of his second, Abiah: they were judges in Beersheba. ³And his sons walked not in his ways, but turned aside after lucre, and took bribes, and perverted judgment.

Prophet Samuel was God-fearing and served God and the people of Israel faithfully. He did justice and never defrauded or oppressed anyone, and all Israel attested to this. However, his sons Joel and Abiah did not walk in the ways of Samuel. They were corrupt and greedy for gains, which caused them to take bribes and pervert judgment. What could have led to this? Maybe Prophet Samuel was too busy with leadership and did not sacrifice the time and resources needed to train his children at the foundational stage. Nonetheless, it could have been because their mother, who is primarily responsible for training and laying a godly foundation for their children, failed to sacrifice the time and resources required at their foundational stage of ages 0 to 7. The focus here is not really on the reason; we have dealt with that in chapter two. The focus is to show that the children of God-fearing parents could be corrupt and ungodly. Therefore, as parents, you should protect your children from the children of your pastors and spiritual leaders of all categories if you truly desire to raise godly children. Just because the parents are godly does not automatically translate to their children being godly. The godly parents may have let their guard down in training their children, and Satan may have taken over. Therefore watch, by their fruits you shall know them. You should only allow a child into your children's lives based on that child's godly character.

Proverbs 20:11

Even a child is known by his doings, whether his work be pure, and whether it be right.

You must protect your children from their cousins. You have to protect them from your nephews and nieces if you truly want to raise godly children. Parents often give unfettered access to their nieces and nephews in their children's lives. They do this because they are their relatives, they are their siblings' children, and they want to maintain family ties. The questions one must ask as a Christian parent are;

1. Do my siblings and I have the same Christian values?
2. If we have the same Christian values, are their children being trained to live by the same values?
3. If so, are their children following and living by the same values?

You may have grown up in a Christian home and received the same godly training as your siblings while growing up. However, you must always evaluate to see if they and their family are still following the same values. This was the grievous mistake King David made, and he paid dearly for it.

2Samuel 13:1-15

¹And it came to pass after this, that Absalom the son of David had a fair sister, whose name was Tamar; and Amnon the son of David loved her. ²And Amnon was so vexed, that he fell sick for his sister Tamar; for she was a virgin; and Amnon thought it hard for him to do any thing to her. ³But Amnon had a friend, whose name was Jonadab, the son of Shimeah David's brother: and Jonadab was a very subtil man. ⁴And he said unto him, Why art thou, being the king's son, lean from day to day? wilt thou not tell me? And Amnon said unto him, I love Tamar, my brother Absalom's sister. ⁵And Jonadab said unto him, Lay thee down on thy bed, and make thyself sick: and when thy father cometh to see thee, say unto him, I pray thee, let my sister Tamar come, and give me meat, and dress the meat in my sight, that I may see it, and eat it at her hand. ⁶So Amnon lay down, and made himself sick: and when the king was come to see him, Amnon said unto the king, I pray thee, let Tamar my sister come, and make me a couple of cakes in my sight, that I may eat at her hand. ⁷Then David sent home to Tamar, saying, Go now to thy brother Amnon's house, and dress him meat. ⁸So Tamar went to her brother Amnon's house; and he was laid down. And she took flour, and kneaded it, and made cakes in his sight, and did bake the cakes. ⁹And she took a pan, and poured them out before him; but he refused to eat. And Amnon said, Have out all men from me. And they went out every man from him. ¹⁰And Amnon said unto Tamar, Bring the meat into the chamber, that I may eat of thine hand. And Tamar took the cakes which she had made, and brought them into the chamber to Amnon her brother. ¹¹And when she had brought them unto him to eat, he took hold of her, and said unto her, Come lie with me, my sister. ¹²And she answered him, Nay, my brother, do not force me; for no such thing ought to be done in Israel: do not thou this folly. ¹³And I, whither shall I cause my shame to go? and as for thee, thou shalt be as one of the fools in Israel. Now therefore, I pray thee, speak unto the king; for he will not withhold me from thee. ¹⁴Howbeit he would not hearken unto her voice: but, being stronger than she, forced her, and lay with her. ¹⁵Then Amnon hated her exceedingly; so that the hatred wherewith he hated her was greater than the love wherewith he had loved her. And Amnon said unto her, Arise, be gone.

King David had a nephew called Jonadab, who was the son of his brother Shimeah, to whom he gave unfettered access to his children because he was a relative. The Bible recorded that Jonadab was very subtle. 2 Samuel 13:3, ***"But Amnon had a friend, whose name was Jonadab, the son of Shimeah David's brother: and Jonadab was a very subtil man."*** This means that Jonadab had the character of Satan. Genesis 3:1, ***"Now the serpent (Satan) was more subtil than any beast of the field which the LORD God had made. And he said unto the woman, Yea, hath God said, Ye shall not eat of every tree of the garden?"*** In other words, Jonadab was the son of Satan. Corrupt Jonadab, the son of Satan, Amnon's cousin deceitfully gave Amnon a strategy that helped him rape his half-sister Tamar who was of the same mother as Absalom. The Bible did not just describe Jonadab as Amnon's cousin but called him his friend. This means that Amnon would have developed lust for Tamar, his sister, because of his friendship with Jonadab. Jonadab must have trained Amnon's illicit sexual appetite for his sister by sharing with him stories of his own secret sexually immoral life with his sisters. This must have been the reason why Amnon was not afraid to share such terrible secret thoughts with him. He must have been used to hearing of Jonadab's own secret illicit sexual escapades before that time. Jonadab was able to corrupt Amnon and help him execute his evil desire to have sex with his sister because they were friends. This evil was possible because King David, the man after God's heart, gave unfettered access to Jonadab the son of Satan, his nephew, into his home and his son's life. King David paid dearly for this error; it cost him his son's life and brought serious chaos to his family.

2Kings 13:28-32

²⁸Now Absalom had commanded his servants, saying, Mark ye now when Amnon's heart is merry with wine, and when I say unto you, Smite Amnon; then kill him, fear not: have not I commanded you? be courageous, and be valiant. ²⁹And the servants of Absalom did unto Amnon as Absalom had commanded. Then all the king's sons arose, and every man gat him up upon his mule, and fled. ³⁰And it came to pass, while they were in the way, that tidings came to David, saying, Absalom hath slain all the king's sons, and there is not one of them left. ³¹Then the king arose, and tare his garments, and lay on the earth; and all his servants stood by with their clothes rent. ³²And Jonadab, the son of Shimeah

David's brother, answered and said, Let not my lord suppose that they have slain all the young men the king's sons; for Amnon only is dead: for by the appointment of Absalom this hath been determined from the day that he forced his sister Tamar.

Now it was the same subtle Jonadab who gave Amnon the evil counsel that led to his death, that gave the perfect storyline of the situation to King David, even amid the chaos and uncertainty of what took place. How did he get to know so perfectly? Was he also involved in helping Absalom hatch out a perfect plan to get Amnon? He spoke without any emotion about what had happened, telling David not to be alarmed that it was only Amnon that died. The Bible says that all these things are written for our learning. Romans 15:4, *"For whatsoever things were written aforetime were written for our learning..."* Christian parents who truly desire to raise godly children for the LORD must learn from King David's mistake/ignorance. This is only shining light on sexual immorality and other consequences that most likely would follow. It may not be a case of murder as seen in David's case, but of the murder of unborn babies through abortions due to unwanted pregnancies. It may also lead to losing your daughter's life in the process of trying to get an abortion. It may lead to losing her life because her cousin, who impregnated her, killed her to cover up the shame of their action. It could also be a case of getting your children initiated into witchcraft or gangs. Parents should not give unfettered access to their nephews and nieces into their homes and children's lives simply because they are their relatives. You may be opening up the door of your family to another subtle Jonadab, the son of Satan.

199

CHAPTER 10

Travail in Prayers for Your Children

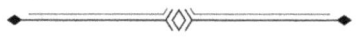

The principles of raising godly children cannot be very effective and lasting without prayers. Notwithstanding the efficacy of all the principles of raising godly children discussed in this book. Without persistent fervent prayers for your children even before they are conceived. All efforts in applying the principles of raising godly children may not produce the desired outcome. The Bible made it clear that by strength shall no man prevail.

1Samuel 2:9

He will keep the feet of his saints, and the wicked shall be silent in darkness; for by strength shall no man prevail.

10:1 The Place of Prayers in Raising Godly Children

Raising godly children unto the LORD is made possible through spiritual battles. Satan, the enemy, is a spiritual being and a wise and powerful one for that matter. While you can overcome earthly things through spiritual means, you cannot overcome spiritual things by carnal means. You cannot prevail over Satan, who is desperate to destroy your children by earthly means alone. You must match fire with fire. Battle that which is spiritual with spiritual weapons. You must contend with Satan spiritually to overcome him in your family. To succeed in raising godly children, you must invite the Spirit of God through fervent, persistent prayers to help you overcome Satan. Raising godly children is not an endeavor of might, knowledge, and wisdom alone but of the Spirit of God and grace. You cannot be with your children 24 hours every day to monitor and direct them, even when they are at home with you, how much more when they are in school. Therefore, you must pray fervently and fast to have your children under the control and leading of the Spirit of God. You must plead with God to give you good children, help you in training them, and keep corrupt peers away from them.

Zechariah 4:6

Then he answered and spake unto me, saying, This is the word of the LORD unto Zerubbabel (your name), saying, Not by might, nor by power, but by my spirit, saith the LORD of hosts.

As an aspiring parent, you must constantly labor for your children in prayers before they are conceived, while they are in the womb, and all the days of their lives. You should plead with God to give you godly children before conceiving them. God can determine their destiny before they are born and can protect them in the womb from being polluted by Satan and his agents. God remains the only one who can guide and guard them 24 hours a day by His Spirit in the secret and the open.

Jeremiah 1:4-5

⁴Then the word of the LORD came unto me, saying, ⁵Before I formed thee in the belly I knew thee; and before thou camest forth out of the womb I sanctified thee, and I ordained thee a prophet unto the nations.

The Almighty God proclaimed that He knew Jeremiah before He formed him in his mother's womb. This means that God purposefully put a prophet in his mother's womb. Jeremiah's parents must have been praying. They must have travailed with God in the place of prayers for a godly child, and God said I will give you a prophet. God also sanctified him in the womb, that is, to set him apart for His own use. This means that God protected him from any satanic pollution in the womb because He has dedicated him as His own. Therefore, Satan could not pollute him or derail his destiny. Before he was born, God ordained him a prophet unto nations. Prophet Jeremiah did not come by chance; his parents must have prayed for him. They must have travailed in prayers and fasting for a godly child. If God knew and foreordained who He was putting in Jeremiah's mother's womb before conception. Then He can answer your prayers for a godly child and deposit him or her in your womb at conception. Has God not said you should ask and it shall be given; seek and you shall find; knock and it shall be opened unto you?

Matthew 7:7-8

7Ask, and it shall be given you; seek, and ye shall find; knock, and it shall be opened unto you: 8For every one that asketh receiveth; and he that seeketh findeth; and to him that knocketh it shall be opened.

The perfect example of asking and travailing in prayers and fasting for a godly child is that of Hannah. She fasted and prayed to God to give her a son and promised to give that child back to God to serve Him all the days of his life. In other words, Hannah was praying for a godly child, because it is only a godly child that can serve the LORD all the days of his life. She asked, sought, and knocked, and the door was opened unto her and she received her request. Hannah travailed in fasting and prayers for a godly child and received the prophet, Samuel.

1Samuel 1:7,9-11,20,26-27

⁷And as he did so year by year, when she went up to the house of the LORD, so she provoked her; therefore she wept, and did not eat ⁹So Hannah rose up after they had eaten in Shiloh, and after they had drunk. Now Eli the priest sat upon a seat by a post of the temple of the LORD. ¹⁰And she was in bitterness of soul, and prayed unto the LORD, and wept sore. ¹¹And she vowed a vow, and said, O LORD of hosts, if thou wilt indeed look on the affliction of thine handmaid, and remember me, and not forget thine handmaid, but wilt give unto thine handmaid a man child, then I will give him unto the LORD all the days of his life, and there shall no razor come upon his head. ²⁰Wherefore it came to pass, when the time was come about after Hannah had conceived, that she bare a son, and called his name Samuel, saying, Because I have asked him of the LORD²⁶And she said, Oh my lord, as thy soul liveth, my lord, I am the woman that stood by thee here, praying unto the LORD. ²⁷For this child I prayed; and the LORD hath given me my petition which I asked of him:

Hannah fasted and prayed earnestly for a godly child, and God heard her prayers. After giving birth, she gave up all that was necessary to spend quality time training the child before sending him to the house of God. Hannah knew that she must perform her duty of training her child before giving him to the Lord as she promised. 1Samuel 1:22, *"But Hannah went not up; for she said unto her husband, I will not go up until the child be weaned, and then I will bring him, that he may appear before the LORD, and there abide for ever."* She denied herself travel, even to the house of God, just to diligently spend time to train her son and pray for him. She knew the importance of early childhood training and prayers. She knew that the training and prayers would form the bedrock of Samuel's life. Because of this, she was willing to sacrifice whatever it would take to lay a solid godly foundation for her son and to establish it through prayers. You can see that godly children do not come by chance. They come through fervent fasting and prayers, and diligence in training.

10:2 There Is Still Hope for The Hopeless

You may have found yourself in an unfortunate situation where your child's or children's foundation has been corrupted and destroyed already. You did not have this knowledge and did not sacrifice time to lay a godly foundation for them through prayers and diligent training. Maybe you did your best in training them the way you know how, but did not do it in the way of the LORD because you were not in the LORD yourself. You may have trained them in the way of the LORD to the best of your knowledge, but not up to the holy standard of the LORD. You may have trained them by the holy standard of God, but neglected the place of prayer. If, by the help of the Holy Spirit, you have now discovered where you did not do well in training your children. Please humble yourself before God in repentance and cry out to Him for help, because He is the only one who can help you and He resists the proud and gives grace to the humble, James 4:6, *"But he giveth more grace. Wherefore he saith, God resisteth the proud, but giveth grace unto the humble."*

Luke 1: 37

For with God nothing shall be impossible.

Jeremiah 32:27

Behold, I am the LORD, the God of all flesh: is there any thing too hard for me?

James 5:16

Confess your faults one to another, and pray one for another, that ye may be healed. The effectual fervent prayer of a righteous man availeth much.

The Bible says that the effectual fervent prayers of the righteous availeth much. It is the prayer of the righteous that availeth much. The potency of prayer rests with the righteousness of the one praying. Even if you are not a righteous parent. You don't know Jesus and have not accepted Him as your Lord and Savior, or maybe you have and you are not living a holy life. You may also be righteous, but now you can see where you failed God in raising your children. You did not focus on training them at their foundational stage of age 0-7. Maybe you did, but did not give much attention to prayers, and Satan seized the occasion to corrupt and destroy their foundation. Now you are in pain and sorrow of heart because of the ungodly lifestyle of your children. The good news is that it is not too late to effect a change, because nothing shall be impossible with God. If only you could acknowledge where you have failed, repent, and reconcile with God. Then begin to labor for them fervently and persistently in prayers and fasting as you continue in righteousness. The Lord will hear you; He will give attention to your prayers and supplications done in righteousness, and deliver your children.

Acts 17:30

And the times of this ignorance God winked at; but now commandeth all men every where to repent:

Acts 16:30-32

³⁰And brought them out, and said, Sirs, what must I do to be saved? ³¹And they said, Believe on the Lord Jesus Christ, and thou shalt be saved, and thy house.

1Peter 3:12

For the eyes of the Lord are over the righteous, and his ears are open unto their prayers: but the face of the Lord is against them that do evil.

Maybe you did a good job raising your children and believe you have no fault for their ungodly ways of life. Nonetheless, persistent fervent prayers and fasting, and supplication are necessary to recover them. The Lord has promised to save the children of the righteous. You may have even trained them by God's holy standard and backed it up with fervent prayers and fasting. However, your child/children have gone astray. Know that there is still hope for the hopeless through persistent, fervent prayers and fasting. You must continue to labor very hard in prayers as a righteous parent, for nothing shall be impossible with God. The effectual fervent prayers of the righteous availeth much. James 5:16, *"... The effectual fervent prayer of a righteous man availeth much."*

Isaiah 49:25

But thus saith the LORD, Even the captives of the mighty shall be taken away, and the prey of the terrible shall be delivered: for I will contend with him that contendeth with thee, and I will save thy children.

The reason why your children are ungodly in their lifestyle is that they have become captives to the mighty. Satan is the mighty and terrible, and he has taken your children as prey. Nonetheless, God promised that even the prey of the mighty, terrible Satan shall be delivered. He said that He will contend with him that is contending with you and save your children. What a great promise from the Almighty God who can do all things. Satan might be the mighty, but God is the Almighty. This means that all powers belong to God, including the powers of the mighty Satan. It means that all authorities and powers are subject to the Almighty God.

Psalms 62:11

God hath spoken once; twice have I heard this; that power belongeth unto God.

Matthew 28:18

And Jesus came and spake unto them, saying, All power is given unto me in heaven and in earth.

Philippians 2:9-10

⁹Wherefore God also hath highly exalted him, and given him a name which is above every name: ¹⁰That at the name of Jesus every knee should bow, of things in heaven, and things in earth, and things under the earth; ¹¹And that every tongue should confess that Jesus Christ is Lord, to the glory of God the Father.

Take hold of the Almighty God in prayers and fasting and plead with Him to deliver your child/children. The Almighty

God, who promised to save your children from the mighty terrible Satan, said that all power in heaven and on earth is in His hands. Call on Jesus today and continue to call on Him to save your children, and in due time, He will surely deliver and save your children from Satan. May the Almighty God increase your faith and strengthen you spiritually and physically. May He release more grace upon you to labor in prayers and fasting for the salvation of your children in Jesus' name, Amen!

10:3 The Efficacy of Persistent Prayers

Psalm 65:2

O thou that hearest prayer, unto thee shall all flesh come.

God is a prayer-answering God. Answering prayers is an attribute of God. It is something He delights in doing. Hearing and answering your prayers gives God great joy. This knowledge should give true Christian parents confidence that God will answer their prayers for their wayward children. Psalm 65:2 says, *"O thou that hearest prayer, unto thee shall all flesh come."* God expects all flesh to come to Him in prayers because He hears prayers, that is, He answers prayers. The question is, did you really go to Him with the burden of your wayward child? If you did, how fervent and persistent were you in your prayers? Many Christian parents give up on their children because they have prayed for many years, and nothing has changed. Instead of getting better, it got worse, so they gave up. They lost faith in their prayers to God. They never understood that God was hearing their prayers and was working out measures in the spiritual that would eventually bring about the physical manifestation of their prayers. However, they gave up before the physical manifestation of their prayers. God wants you to persistently come to Him in prayers because it gives Him pleasure. God derives pleasure in seeing His children exercise enduring faith in Him, so that He will do what they are praying for. Jesus taught us, His followers, lessons on the efficacy of persistent prayers.

Luke 11:5-10

⁵And he said unto them, Which of you shall have a friend, and shall go unto him at midnight, and say unto him, Friend, lend me three loaves; ⁶For a friend of mine in his journey is come to me, and I have nothing to set before him? ⁷And he from within shall answer and say, Trouble me not: the door is now shut, and my children are with me in bed; I cannot rise and give thee. ⁸I say unto you, Though he will not rise and give him, because he is his friend, yet because of his importunity he will rise and give him as many as he needeth. ⁹And I say unto you, Ask, and it shall be given you; seek, and ye shall find; knock, and it shall be opened unto you. ¹⁰For every one that asketh receiveth; and he that seeketh findeth; and to him that knocketh it shall be opened.

Jesus said that though the man would not respond to his friend because of friendship, he would surely respond to his request because of his importunity (persistence). Luke 11:8, *"I say unto you, Though he will not rise and give him, because he is his friend, yet because of his importunity he will rise and give him as many as he needeth."* It was Jesus – God in human flesh that revealed the efficacy of persistent prayers to believers. In this parable of Jesus, the man in need persistently disturbed his friend, asking and knocking so that his friend could not rest. When the friend saw that his friend was not going to give him rest, he was forced to get up and give him all that he needed. Has God not commanded us to do the same to Him?

Isaiah 62:6-7

⁶I have set watchmen upon thy walls, O Jerusalem, which shall never hold their peace day nor night: ye that make mention of the LORD, keep not silence, ⁷And give him no rest, till he establish, and till he make Jerusalem a praise in the earth

God commanded those who make mention of the LORD; that is, those who call upon the LORD in prayers, to not keep silent and give him no rest. Just like that man who had a visitor at midnight knocked persistently, disturbing his friend to lend him some loaves until he got what he needed. God had already said that His children should give Him no rest until they receive all they need. Isaiah 62:7, *"...ye that make mention of the LORD, keep not silence, ⁷And give him no rest, till he establish, and till he make Jerusalem a praise in the earth"* In other words, you that is calling upon God to save your wayward children; keep not silence, and give Him no rest, till He establish and make you children a praise in the earth. Persistent prayers are proof of your faith in God. Persistent prayer is faith in God in action; the belief that God can do what you are praying for. It reflects your faith in God that, though it may take a long time, you are persuaded that God will surely answer you. Faith is the currency required to purchase all that we need from God. Without it, it's impossible to please God or receive from Him.

Hebrews 11:1,6

¹Now faith is the substance of things hoped for, the evidence of things not seen. ⁶But without faith it is impossible to please him: for he that cometh to God must believe that he is, and that he is a rewarder of them that diligently seek him.

James 1:6-7

⁶But let him ask in faith, nothing wavering. For he that wavereth is like a wave of the sea driven with the wind and tossed. ⁷For let not that man think that he shall receive any thing of the Lord.

Persistent prayers stir up and maintain the faith required to receive from God. Jesus also shed more light on this very fact with another parable. In this parable, Jesus taught Christians the correlation between persistent prayers and faith.

Luke 18:1-8

¹And he spake a parable unto them to this end, that men ought always to pray, and not to faint; ²Saying, There was in a city a judge, which feared not God, neither regarded man: ³And there was a widow in that city; and she came unto him, saying, Avenge me of mine adversary. ⁴And he would not for a while: but afterward he said within himself, Though I fear not God, nor regard man; ⁵Yet because this widow troubleth me, I will avenge her, lest by her continual coming she weary me. ⁶And the Lord said, Hear what the unjust judge saith. ⁷And shall not God avenge his own elect, which cry day and night unto him, though he bear long with them? ⁸I tell you that he will avenge them speedily.

211

Nevertheless when the Son of man cometh, shall he find faith on the earth?

Jesus told this parable to make believers understand the efficacy of persistent prayers and its connection with the believer's faith. The parable teaches believers to pray always and not lose faith. The widow's persistence in asking the wicked judge to avenge her adversary was so powerful. Although the wicked judge did not want to help her, the power of her continuous asking and coming back to ask broke him down, and he succumbed to helping her. The wicked judge said, *"⁵Yet because this widow troubleth me, I will avenge her, lest by her continual coming she weary me."* Then Jesus said, *"⁷And shall not God avenge his own elect, which cry day and night unto him, though he bear long with them?"* Jesus is saying that if persistent petitioning could weary a wicked judge to change his mind to help the widow. How much more effective will your persistent prayers be in moving the good God who said; Give me no rest with your prayers? He is saying how will God, your Father, not be moved with your persistent prayers to avenge you of Santan and rescue your wayward child from him. The persistent petitioning of the widow was proof of her faith in the judge's ability to solve her problem. Her persistence demonstrated her faith in what she was doing. Her persistence shows that she believed without a shadow of a doubt that what she was doing would eventually pay off, no matter how long it took. This shows the direct correlation between persistent prayers and faith. Jesus alluded to this when He ended the parable with this question in verse 8, *"Nevertheless when the Son of man cometh, shall he find faith on the earth?"* This parable emphasized the efficacy of persistent prayers as an exercise of faith in the Almighty God. Matthew 15:22-28 tells the story of a woman who used persistent prayers to demonstrate her faith in Jesus's authority to deliver her daughter from the devil.

Matthew 15:22-28

22And, behold, a woman of Canaan came out of the same coasts, and cried unto him, saying, Have mercy on me, O Lord, thou Son of David; my daughter is grievously vexed with a devil. 23But he answered her not a word. And his disciples came and besought him, saying, Send her away; for she crieth after us. 24But he answered and said, I am not sent but unto the lost sheep of the house of Israel. 25Then came she and worshipped him, saying, Lord, help me. 26But he answered and said, It is not meet to take the children's bread, and to cast it to dogs. 27And she said, Truth, Lord: yet the dogs eat of the crumbs which fall from their masters' table. 28Then Jesus answered and said unto her, O woman, great is thy faith: be it unto thee even as thou wilt. And her daughter was made whole from that very hour.

This woman earnestly prayed to Jesus persistently to rescue her daughter from the devil. The devil had hijacked her daughter. Jesus never complained about the woman's continuous asking; He was not wearied by it. It was His disciples who were complaining that she was disturbing them. You cannot weary God by your perpetual prayers; keep on asking. Though Jesus kept quiet for a while, verse 23, **"But he answered her not a word"**. Nonetheless, He was hearing the woman's prayers. You may not have heard a word from God concerning your prayers for your child/children hijacked by the devil. Persist in your prayers, He is hearing you. He is only wanting to prove your faith in Him. At last, Jesus answered her, praised her great faith, and rescued her daughter from the grip of Satan. Matthew 15:28, *"Then Jesus answered and said unto her, O woman, great is thy faith: be it unto thee even as thou wilt. And her daughter was made whole from that very hour."* Have faith in God, persist in your prayers and in due time Jesus will deliver your children for the bondage of Satan. Isaiah 62:7, *"...ye that make mention of the LORD, keep not silence, 7And give him no rest, till he establish, and till he make Jerusalem a praise in the earth"* In other words, you that is calling upon God to save your wayward children; keep not silence, and give Him no rest, till He establish and make your children a praise in the earth. Amen.

Other Books Written by The Author

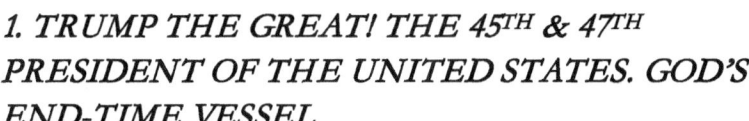

1. TRUMP THE GREAT! THE 45ᵀᴴ & 47ᵀᴴ PRESIDENT OF THE UNITED STATES. GOD'S END-TIME VESSEL

Amazon Book Reviews On Trump The Great!

1. Angel59: Second coming of Christ

This book opened my eyes to how close our lord Jesus is coming soon. The current events are just the beginning of what's to come.

2. Lala: Very Insightful, Second Coming Of Jesus Christ!

Just finished this book, great read!

The storytelling, insight, humor, humility, and scriptural relations in the writing are remarkable. The style of writing is engaging, I love the way the book ended, the very last page.

We choose you, President Donald J Trump!

TRUMPITO we stand with you! Much love from New Jersey! #MAGA #TRUMPFOREVERYONE

WHEN JESUS SAYS YES NOBODY CAN SAY NO!

THE KINGDOM OF GOD IS AT HAND, REPENT AND WALK WITH THE LORD IN HOLINESS AND RIGHTEOUSNESS TODAY!

3. Kindle Customer: The expectations of the righteous shall not be cut off

This is a striking representation and cover. The title says it all. God is truly at work, and anyone who knows that there is a creator and men are the creatures should venture to read this book. A well-thought-out book that flows with the sequence.

4. OG: Wow!

This indeed is the revelation of God to His children. Never in my years of reading the Bible have I understood the excerpt of scriptures cited in this book; the 7 days of creation and its relation to the time of Christ coming. I am baffled at the author's understanding of the scripture, and I am convinced that this is the Lord's doing. Indeed, He revealed secret things to them that fear Him. This is a strong wake-up call to me and Christians who await the rapture. It is all a cry unto sinners to come to Christ. I am blessed beyond words! I started this book as I woke up this morning because I had the burden to read it since yesterday for what reason, I don't know, but now I know. I started reading this book and never dropped it till I finished it, I never wanted it to finish. This is a great evangelism tool. God bless the author, Pastor Cliff McAnthony. More grace! Maranatha!

5. Roxen Herman: A Must Read!

Very insightful and scripturally accurate. I highly recommend purchasing this book, you won't be disappointed.

2. THE STORY OF JESUS COLORING BOOK

Amazon Book Reviews on The Story of Jesus Coloring Book.

1. Chidu: Buy it and enjoy it

Children and adults alike would enjoy the simple easy to follow truth of God's word.

3. THE STORY OF DANIEL COLORING BOOK

4. KIDIFFIED

Amazon Book Reviews on KIDDIFIED.

1. Sonia: GET THIS BOOK NOW

This OUTSTANDING *book presents a provocative and deeply spiritual perspective on the influence of modern culture on children. It challenges parents to rethink the seemingly harmless terminology we use to refer to our children, such as calling them "kids" — a term that, may unconsciously link them to symbolic associations with goats, sin offerings, and even Satanic practices. Reading this book shows you how, Satan has infiltrated the nurturing environment meant to guide children in godliness, instead turning them into "kiddified" souls disconnected from God.*

This book posits that modern media — including social media, music, TV, cartoons, and video games — serves as a vehicle for spiritual harm, conditioning children to be rebellious, selfish, and indifferent to the divine. One of the book's core messages is that parents need to take back control over their children's upbringing, particularly during the most formative years. The author urges parents to be vigilant in guarding their children's hearts and minds against the pernicious influence of secularism, materialism, and Satanic ideologies. The author challenges readers to reconsider the sources of influence in their children's lives and to actively cultivate a spiritual environment where children can grow in their faith and knowledge of God.

Ultimately, this book is a wake-up call for Christian parents, urging them to evaluate how they are raising their children in a world filled with distractions and subtle spiritual dangers. I WILL HIGHLY RECOMMEND THIS TO EVERYONE.

2. Gabriel: A diagnostic, problem-solving masterpiece!

I highly recommend this book. They say, a problem discovered is a problem half-solved.

As a school teacher, I see firsthand the effect of words on children. Words are prophetic. They can build up a life or tear it down.

If every parent, leader, carer, adult, and child (those that can read) in our world reads this book and makes the necessary, recommended changes to their vocabulary and practices, our world will be a way better place!

I highly recommend this book!